STOLEN YEARS

STOLEN YEARS

STORIES OF THE WRONGFULLY IMPRISONED

REUVEN FENTON

with the last written words of Rubin "The Hurricane" Carter

Tantor
media
A DIVISION OF RECORDED BOOKS

To Marty and Daniel

Tantor Media, Inc.
A Division of Recorded Books
6 Business Park Road
Old Saybrook, CT 06475

tantor.com
tantorpublishing.com

Stolen Years: Stories of the Wrongfully Imprisoned

Author photo © Paul Martinka
Select cover photos provided courtesy of Muhammad Don Ray Adams,
Debra Brown, Cornelius Dupree, and Thomas Kennedy.
Design and Illustrations by Elizabeth Gibbings.

ISBN: 9781630150013
Printed in the United States of America
First Tantor Media Printing, November 10, 2015

Contents

FOREWORD

March 2014

When, at the age of twenty-nine, I was wrongly convicted of a triple murder in Paterson, New Jersey, I just narrowly escaped the electric chair. I was given life in prison instead.

Because I might have been executed for something I didn't do, I have staunchly opposed capital punishment to this day. Who knows how many people have been executed for crimes they did not commit? In an imperfect system run by human beings (and what system isn't?) errors are inevitable. Capital punishment is a perfect punishment—an eye for an eye—but you cannot have a perfect punishment in an imperfect system.

Nothing illustrates the imperfection of the system more than wrongful convictions. They are the absolute bane of the justice system.

In this gripping book, Reuven Fenton shows us the devastating consequences that arise when one is convicted for a crime he or she did not commit.

These stories have happy endings. Sadly, most do not.

The causes of miscarriages of justice crop up again and again. A case is not safe in the presence of overworked and poorly prepared defense attorneys; false science; the youth of a defendant and his or her criminal history; racial prejudice; unreliable eyewitnesses; and, especially, the absence of hard evidence proving the defendant is innocent.

Many of these cases become constructs of the prosecutors—damning stories that may persuade a jury to convict while the defense attorney is asleep at the wheel. And this is where the real problem lies. Every officer of the court is ethically bound to the truth, but not every officer of the court can resist the urge to further his or her career with a string of convictions, whether or not these convictions comply with the truth. It is precisely when winning or losing becomes the be-all and end-all that truth is disregarded and justice becomes elusive.

I disagree with those who say tunnel vision by prosecutors causes wrongful convictions. *Tunnel vision* sounds like a disease or condition that prosecutors suffer from and cannot control. The only one suffering is the convicted person.

My view is that the real cause of wrongful convictions is willful blindness. And that's something most defendants never imagine is possible. People like Cornelius Dupree naively believed "the truth would set you free." Truth, my friend, wouldn't be recognized if she sashayed into the courtroom and sat smack-dab in the judge's lap.

Once the defendant is found guilty, the real problems start. He or she is now buried under a deep, deep pile of procedural shit. That shit is there to protect the conviction and the people who perpetrated it. It sometimes takes decades to dig oneself out, but not without DNA evidence or another murderer or rapist admitting to the crime. "A body for a body," as district attorneys like to say. Even then, it's no slam dunk.

So the ambitions and reputations of the legal officers play a huge role in the failings of the system. That's why we hear about Brady violations—instances in which prosecutors deliberately hide evidence favorable to a defendant. And the prosecutors often do it *post-conviction*. Why would they do such a thing if not to protect the reputations of the people who conspired in the original conviction?

I see a world where reputations are enhanced by admitting to error and by working for the truth. The system would not be perfect but it would sure be a whole lot better.

What, then, do men and women do when they are sent to prison for something they have not done? To every human being in prison, guilty or innocent, I would say that it all depends upon attitude. The physical body is the vehicle in which we traverse life, but our attitude is our steering wheel.

In prison, people find themselves at the bottom of human existence. What a prisoner must say is, "OK, whatever I've done in life has led me to where I am today. Therefore, if I want to get out of prison and stay out, I've got to turn around and go back the other way."

Prisoners must use this time to learn how to read if they don't know how, to learn to write, to learn a skill if they never had one. Maybe on the outside they didn't have time for any of these things. Now they do. This time has been imposed upon them. They must use it to look at themselves, to make themselves indispensable, to awaken.

I see myself in some of the former inmates profiled in the pages of this book—like Devon Ayers of the Bronx, who wrongfully went to prison for murder. "Prison changed me into a better person," he says, and I know what he means. Although it wasn't the foul prison that did it; it was Devon.

That being said, self-improvement is the prisoner's responsibility; the prisoner's responsibility has nothing to do with the awesome responsibility of those who run the system. What is their responsibility? To just aim for the truth; not a conviction, not a verdict, not a win, nor a loss. Just the truth.

If the conviction was found to be wrong, they must recognize it and admit it. They must not fool themselves into believing that protecting a wrongful conviction serves justice, truth, or anything but themselves. If they reduce the barriers to the truth, they will relieve terrible human suffering, individual by individual. That's a good thing. Take it from me, prison is suffering, and prison without justice is crucifixion.

To live in a world where truth matters and justice—however late—really happens would be heaven right here on earth. Heaven on earth.

Dr. Rubin "Hurricane" Carter
May 6, 1937–April 20, 2014

PREFACE

"Go to the precinct."

Those are all the instructions a reporter at a New York City tabloid needs to hear from an editor to know that he or she has been assigned a perp walk.

A perp walk is when cops walk the accused out of the station house in cuffs and put him in a squad car to take him to court. It's a quick and chaotic mess. Photographers try not to trip over each other as they attempt to get a decent shot, while the reporters shout questions at the perp from the outer edges of the scrum.

I've been assigned perp walks for as long as I've been a reporter for the greatest tabloid in the world, the *New York Post*.

The walks are almost always preceded by hours of waiting, as detectives work the perp over and over in an interrogation room. If it's a particularly high-profile case—someone collared for pushing some poor guy onto the subway tracks right before the E train barreled past, for instance—then a lot of other reporters and camera people wait with you.

Empty coffee cups pile up at our feet. The wind shifts. Precinct detectives start giving us little nods when they come outside for smoke breaks. Representatives from the NYPD's public information office show up.

And then it happens.

Flanked by a detective on each side, the perp exits the station and walks down the steps into a tidal wave of flashing lights and reporters belting out questions like, "Why did you do it?"

Usually he keeps his head down and says nothing. But sometimes he looks straight into the throng. I've seen a few perps smile, like they're enjoying their fifteen seconds of fame.

And every once in a while they say a few words: "I didn't do nothing!"

When it's all over, the consensus among the reporters and cameramen is, "Yeah, sure you didn't."

There's an assumption when someone gets arrested—especially for something really grim, like murder or child molestation—that the accused is guilty. You look at the person's mug shot, see those bleary eyes and messed-up hair, and say to yourself, "Guilty." It's human intuition.

Often, this intuition is spot-on. Some crimes happen in front of dozens of witnesses, or are caught on surveillance tapes. Sometimes the perpetrator's fingerprints are all over the crime scene. Sometimes he's caught with the victim's blood literally on his hands.

But sometimes there are no witnesses, and no solid evidence to match the accused to the crime. And it eats at you, as you wonder *just what if* the perp is innocent? Because innocent or not, they all bury their faces in their hands the same way when they hear the jury foreman say, "Guilty." Nobody, not even a cold-blooded killer, wants to sit in prison for the rest of his life.

On the flip side, stories I'm getting assigned increasingly often these days are about exonerations. It's a whole event. Reporters pack the courtroom to catch the look on the inmate's face as the judge tells him, "You are free to go." And then comes the best part, when he walks to the gallery and tearfully embraces his now-grown children for the first time as a free man.

At the press conference afterward, the delirious exoneree

tries to field questions that are impossible to answer in a sound bite.

"How does it feel to be free?" they'll ask.

"It feels amazing," he'll say.

But I always want to know more. I want to know how awful the prison food was and how tiny the cells were and how much the prison scrubs itched. And how did it feel when his kids stopped visiting and answering his letters? And what was it like trying to rebuild a life from scratch after getting thrust back into a world that had changed so much?

This book is my attempt to answer those questions and many others, through the voices of ten remarkable individuals who've been to the worst kind of hell and back. These men and women bared their souls to me and opened my eyes to the horrible plight of the incarcerated innocent.

I have been as thorough a scribe as possible, quoting these folks extensively from hundreds of hours of interviews. I have culled additional material for this book from thousands of pages of court documents and media reports, as well as from information provided to me by the lawyers who represented these extraordinary people. I hope I have given them their due.

I owe these ten exonerees an enormous debt of gratitude for their patience as I peppered them with endless questions that ranged from the philosophical to the mundane. Several of them told me they'd started having nightmares again from reliving the horror with me.

But their stories need to be told.

INTRODUCTION

For nineteen-year-old Cornelius Dupree, the skip from freedom to lockup was so fast, so sudden, so *random*, that the reality didn't sink in until he was known as inmate #308310.

The Dallas teen had been walking with a friend to a party when the two were stopped and frisked by police officers looking for suspects in a robbery-rape case. Dupree and his friend were arrested, falsely identified as the perpetrators, charged, jailed, tried, convicted, and finally sentenced to sixty years in prison. From the day he was arrested, Dupree didn't know freedom for thirty-one years.

Drayton Witt was still mourning the passing of his five-month-old adopted son Steven when cops arrested the Arizona man for shaking the child to death. At trial it didn't seem to matter that Steven had been in and out of the hospital for seizures since birth. Nor did it matter that the incriminating medical research on shaken baby syndrome was dubious at best. Witt did ten years behind bars.

Debra Brown, a Utah mother of three, took a drive one day to check on her ailing buddy Lael. She found him dead from a gunshot wound to the head and called the cops, hysterical. The ensuing investigation found Brown to be the chief suspect because…well, she and Lael had hung out a lot, she had the key to his house, and she'd swung by with soup the day before she found his body. No actual evidence connected her to the crime. She was locked up for eighteen years.

That's how these things go sometimes.

The stories in this book are about your worst nightmare come to life. The kind of nightmare where one day you're just a face in the crowd, and the next you're notorious, wearing jail scrubs and sitting in a cell waiting to be tried.

And it just gets worse from there.

The stories presented here are full of heartbreak and betrayal and violence. But more than anything, they are about hope and redemption, about ten amazing people who fended off the blackest kind of despair to keep fighting for freedom.

These ten exonerees are among the more than 1,400 people who were released from prison since 1989 after being found wrongfully convicted. There's no doubt that this is just a small fraction of innocent people who have been incarcerated during that time. Still, it's encouraging that the number of exonerations has increased annually. There were twenty-one exonerations in 1989, and ninety-one in 2013.

The increase is owed to the growing number of innocence organizations springing up across the country. Each exoneration brings more awareness to the problem, which gets more public eyes focused on the police and prosecutors whose overly aggressive tactics, bad evidence, or misconduct put innocent people away.

As you're reading this, an impossible-to-document number of wrongly convicted people are sitting in prison, and only a small fraction will ever get out. If this book helps fuel a burgeoning conversation about lives destroyed by our win-at-all-costs criminal justice system, I've done my job.

Chapter 1

DAMON THIBODEAUX
Louisiana, 15 Years

Damon Thibodeaux yawns.

It's six in the morning and he's just woken from a dreamless sleep. He gazes at the ceiling for a few seconds before hoisting himself up.

It's so cramped in here, putting on a shirt and pants is a Harry Houdini magic trick. The walls barely fit his five-foot-nine, square-shouldered body. He's a doberman living in a doghouse built for a dachshund.

Once dressed and washed up, he sits and gazes ahead. He cracks a smile.

Because he is so tickled by what he does *not* see: a concrete wall with steel bars in the foreground.

Instead, through the windshield of his truck he sees a sky so brilliantly blue it's the very color of exhilaration. And where the sky meets the horizon, asphalt—beautiful, sparkling, and stretching for a thousand miles.

After a quick breakfast eaten high in the driver's seat of his big rig, he turns the key, puts his foot on the clutch and shifts into gear—and starts watching the world unfold. For Thibodeaux, the best scenery is the kind that's always moving.

"I've seen just about every state in the continental US," he says. "I've been over the Rockies, what, seven, eight, times?

The view never gets boring. I've been through Arizona, Nevada, over the Appalachians, the Ozarks.

"They call it hauling freight, but as far as I'm concerned I get paid to travel the country."

For fifteen years, nothing moved. Thibodeaux was a death row inmate in solitary confinement at Louisiana State Penitentiary—better known as "Angola," or "Alcatraz of the South"—where days bore little difference from weeks, and weeks from months, and months from years. Thibodeaux calls that time "one big black hole" in his life.

"The thing is, a lot of guys try to fill that hole," Thibodeaux says. "I'm not gonna try to fill it because you can't fill it…it's just gone."

What he chooses to do is look ahead. And he can think of no better vantage point than the one he's at right now. Sure, the truck's cab makes for a cramped night's sleep. And maybe it is sort of cell-like in here. But who cares? In prison it was the involuntary confinement—the inability to step outside to so much as take a piss in the bushes—that man was never meant to endure.

It was 1996, and Damon Thibodeaux felt free as a bird.

He was twenty-two and working as a deckhand on a Mississippi River tugboat. He labored from noon to midnight mopping the deck, securing the barge, making sure the lines were in good order. And when things had quieted down he'd sit on the barge and watch the stars.

No worries, no plans, except maybe getting a pilot's license so he could captain the boat himself one day. Thibodeaux had recently come back to his hometown of New Orleans after a decade of living in Midland, Texas. When a cousin hooked him up with the deckhand job, he was glad he made the move.

One Friday afternoon in July, while on leave from duty,

Thibodeaux visited some distant cousins, the Champagnes, in a suburb of New Orleans. One of the cousins, fourteen-year-old Crystal, asked him for a ride to the Winn-Dixie supermarket to buy some groceries. He didn't feel like it, so she went by herself.

She didn't come back.

Her mother went looking for her, then her father. As the hours passed, others joined the effort, including Thibodeaux. They started with the most obvious places, the shopping center and the park where she played softball, but still no sign of Crystal. Then they expanded the search perimeter.

After nearly twenty-four hours of nonstop searching, an exhausted Thibodeaux went home to catch a few hours' sleep. He threw himself into bed and was just drifting off when he heard a pounding on his door. It was detectives from the Jefferson Parish sheriff's office. They wanted to ask him some questions at the office.

Right around the time Thibodeaux arrived at the sheriff's, a family friend named John Tomlinson found Crystal. She was dead, her body in some brush by a bridge on a bank of the Mississippi. A red wire was wrapped around her neck, her skull was fractured, and one of her front teeth had been knocked out.

When word came back to the sheriff's about Crystal's death, Thibodeaux felt something shift in the air. The detectives, who'd been civil and professional to that point, turned hostile. "Where were you the night Crystal disappeared?" they asked. "What were you doing that night? Did you rape her? Did you kill her?"

"No," he said, and they called him a liar and started all over again. Hours passed as the pressure mounted. The detectives tried to bait Thibodeaux, claiming his cousins denied he was ever at their apartment the night Crystal disappeared. Thibodeaux thought he'd asphyxiate when he heard that.

The cops described the pain he'd feel when his body succumbed to lethal injection to pay for what he did.

His brain felt like it was melting.

Then came the final blow: they strapped Thibodeaux to a lie detector test, threw question after question at him, and then announced he'd failed the test.

With that, Thibodeaux passed out. "That's the point where I realized I was never gonna walk out of here," he would say years later.[1]

By 4 a.m., the interrogation had seeped into its ninth hour and Thibodeaux's endurance ran out. Delirious with fear, exhaustion, and hunger, he confessed to killing Crystal. "At that point I was tired," he would later tell a reporter during an interview. "I was hungry. All I wanted to do was sleep, and I was willing to tell them anything they wanted me to tell them if it would get me out of that interrogation room."[2]

He spewed out a confession that was just a regurgitation of what detectives had fed him: he'd taken Crystal under the bridge. She wanted sex and Thibodeaux was happy to oblige, but when he got too rough and Crystal begged him to stop, he punched and choked her, and eventually strangled her to death with a wire from his car speaker.

"I didn't know that I had done it, but I done it," he told his interrogators.[3]

Signed confession in hand, the detectives charged Thibodeaux with murder. A few hours later, when he came to his senses, he recanted everything. But the sheriff's department wasn't handing back its prize, not even after investigators quickly unearthed details so contradictory to Thibodeaux's confession that he ought to have been sent home that very day—with an apology and a fruit basket to boot.

The wire around Crystal's neck was a red electrical conductor wire, not the speaker wire from Thibodeaux's car that he confessed to killing her with. And, contrary to what the detectives had told Thibodeaux, Crystal's mother Dawn told police he *was* in her apartment when her daughter had gone to the grocery store. (At his trial, Dawn changed her story and testified that he was not in her apartment after all. Years later, she claimed she couldn't remember whether he was there or not.)

As he waited in jail, new holes kept forming in his confession. The autopsy revealed that Crystal had been hit in the face with a blunt object, not Thibodeaux's fist, as he'd claimed. And the forensic examiner found that Crystal had not had sex for at least twenty-four hours before she died.

No sex, no punch to the face, no speaker wire. Yet at trial, the state found creative ways to plug up those holes. In one wild instance, an expert witness explained that the lack of evidence of sex could be attributed to maggots that ate up any traces of Thibodeaux's semen.

Meanwhile, prosecutors painted Thibodeaux as a troubled young man from a broken home. Just the kind of damaged screwup who would not only defile a fourteen-year-old sexually, but would kill her in cold blood. They also brought in two witnesses who had identified Thibodeaux in the photo lineup as a man they'd seen standing nervously near the murder scene.

Thibodeaux's attorney, meanwhile, put up an uninspired defense that inexplicably failed to explain to jurors that the confession, the key piece of evidence, had been false. Thibodeaux learned later on that the attorney, a former detective, had never defended a murder case before. What's more, he was applying for a job in the District Attorney's office at the time of the trial.

Nevertheless, Thibodeaux was confident that the jury would acquit and this nightmare would end. But on October 3, 1997, after a mere forty-five minutes of deliberations, the jury filed into the courtroom and the foreman read the verdict: "Guilty."

"I was flabbergasted," Thibodeaux says. "I was like, 'Weren't you people paying attention?' Even now it shocks me that people were so inattentive at my trial."

The next day, the jury recommended he be sentenced to death. The *New Orleans Times Picayune* story from that day was headlined, "Rapist, Killer Gets Death; Man Murdered Teen Stepcousin." It quoted Crystal's father Clifton as saying he was "glad" for Thibodeaux's death sentence, "He deserved it. He beat my daughter so bad in the face, it's unreal."

Thibodeaux sat in the Jefferson Parish county jail for three weeks, awaiting final word on whether the judge would accept the jury's recommendation—but he was pretty much resigned to the inevitable. "It wasn't so much, *Oh my God, I'm gonna die!* as *How am I going to survive this?*" he recalls thinking. "I knew I had my appeals, but my question was what's this going to be like if the justice system failed in such a terrible way? I just had a jury completely ignore the case. How am I going to prove to someone else that I didn't do it when these people who weren't paying attention think that I did?"

Thibodeaux was brought back to court on a Friday for sentencing. Judge Patrick McCabe asked him to stand. Then he sentenced him to death—on grounds that society could not tolerate murderers of children.

"It's kind of a surreal moment," Thibodeaux says. "You watch helplessly as your life's ripped away from you and there's nothing you can do about it."

Looking back all these years later, he still can't believe

that the prosecutors, those dignified servants of the state, had played the court like frat boys playing foosball. "You assume that professionals, people who have gone to law school and trained to do this, wouldn't just blatantly rip someone's life apart just because they want to win," he says.

That night, a deputy sheriff put Thibodeaux in a squad car and set out for Louisiana State Penitentiary—a two-and-a-half-hour drive. The sky was clear, and Thibodeaux watched the stars the entire ride. "All I could think about was am I going to see the stars again? I could have thought about a hundred other things, like my life, and why I had ended up here. But all I could think about was the night sky."

Louisiana State Penitentiary, nicknamed "Angola" after the town it's in, sits at the end of State Highway 66. It spans twenty-eight square miles, large enough to fit five Louisiana State University campuses. Bordered on three sides by the Mississippi River, there is nowhere to run but out the front gate.

There's an odd beauty to the grassy, well-kept grounds, which include a golf course for employees and a ten-thousand-seat stadium built for the biannual Angola Rodeo, an event that attracts multitudes. There's a farm on the property, too. Angola opened in 1901 on land that had once been home to four slave plantations. The symbolism of that bit of history is not lost on the prisoners who work those fields today. They call it "the Last Slave Plantation."

Death row inmates are exempt from such grueling work—or from doing any work at all. For twenty-three hours a day they are locked up with no human contact. They get one hour a day outside the cell, which they use to take a shower, make a phone call, or walk up and down the tier. "You have no life. You just exist," Thibodeaux says. "Death row is solitary confinement, completely. Every time you see someone, there's always a set of bars between you and them."

It took two and a half years before Thibodeaux met his appeals lawyer, and during that time he slept and watched TV and did nothing else. If he remembers a single one of those nine-hundred-some-odd days, he remembers them all. "Television was the only way I could deal with the excessive boredom. There was *nothing to do*."

The TVs hung from the wall across from the cells, one to every four inmates. Thibodeaux favored sci-fi shows like *Babylon 5* and *Doctor Who*. But he was particularly into *Star Trek* in all its incarnations: *Voyager, Enterprise, Deep Space Nine, The Next Generation,* and the classic 1960s episodes that aired in the morning.

Thibodeaux would have to coordinate with his neighbors to work out a TV schedule. Some liked to watch sports all the time. Others liked to watch game shows or soap operas or reality shows. If you had a station that aired your show twice a day, you might let another inmate watch his show and you'd watch yours later.

Sometimes this didn't work out and guys would get angry and curse at each other. Sometimes they'd get so mad they'd fling their own shit at each other. "When something like that happened, the guards were not nice," Thibodeaux says. "They had to send an inmate orderly down to clean up the mess. They cracked down pretty hard on people who did stuff like that."

To be fair, Thibodeaux did a few things besides sleeping and watching TV. He'd clean his six-by-nine-foot cell twice a day, wiping down the jail bars, the sink and toilet, straightening out his little desk, and making his bed. Officers didn't like messy cells, and if they found a mess they'd take your stuff. Thibodeaux didn't have much to take. His footlocker held a toothbrush, three pairs of jeans, three or four sweatshirts, T-shirts, boxers, and socks. In time, a pile of legal work would start to form off to the side and eventually grow to some two-thousand pages.

During his daily hour outside the cell, he'd pace back and forth on the tier. He smoked too much and his slender frame grew flabby from the high-fat, high-sodium prison food. It was always rice-and-gravy-based grub: boiled hamburger patties in gravy, cooked turkey in gravy, beef in gravy, chicken in gravy. The one saving grace was the availability of greens grown on the farm.

Every now and then a fight would break out on the tiers—at least they called them fights. The bars separating inmates only allowed for lightning-quick, single-strike attacks. "I've seen guys boil stuff in the microwave and throw it on other guys," Thibodeaux says. "I've seen guys standing by the bars and someone walked by and cut them with something. You probably can't kill someone on death row, but you can do some harm to him."

After an attack, the administration would rotate inmates to new cells. Thibodeaux always prayed to God that he would be given a cell with a fan in front of it. "The temperatures were astronomical," he says. "We would sometimes strip down to our boxers and sleep on the floor, which was not a whole lot cooler, maybe two or three degrees, but preferable.

"The mattress was some type of fire retardant foam-type stuff wrapped in plastic. You can imagine how hot that was, how sticky it would get. Every night I would wake up in a pool of sweat because it was so hot. The mattress would be soaked."

In the summertime, Thibodeaux only got about an hour's sleep each night. He'd baste like a slow-roasting turkey as he listened to the radio and stared out the window. The heat problem was so bad that eventually, in 2013, three death row inmates sued the penitentiary and the Louisiana Department of Public Safety and Corrections for the excessive heat, alleging that in one year, temperatures reached 195 degrees.

Monday through Saturday, Thibodeaux's life was about being drenched in sweat and nearly comatose with depression.

Sunday was that too, plus something far worse. On Sundays, Angola let the tourists in to death row—moms and dads and gaping-eyed kids who'd come to stare at this morbidly fascinating bunch of Hannibal Lecters.

Before the tour began corrections officers would instruct visitors on safety measures, "Each and every inmate here is on death row for murder and is considered highly dangerous. For your safety, do not walk close to the bars." The inmates were ordered in advance to keep their mouths shut as the families asked the tour guides questions like, "What's this one in for? Why are they allowed to wear regular clothes? Shouldn't they be in jumpsuits?"

"I'd see fear and hatred in their eyes and I couldn't say anything," Thibodeaux recalls.

"We're not monkeys in a zoo. We're human beings. I get it if they're bringing law students down to the tiers to meet their future clients, or schoolkids, 'Hey, look, this is what happens if you kill somebody.' But the idea of tours to the general public for profit? It's beyond sick."

When the tourists came, Thibodeaux tried to make like a tiger at the zoo and just ignore them.

But it was impossible.

Early on in his sentence, Thibodeaux had listlessly filed his appeals, not because he thought it would help but because that's what inmates do. But two and a half years into prison, he made a resolution that he was ready to die. "I decided being on death row was a fate worse than death," he says. "There were guys around me who'd been on death row for twenty, twenty-five years. I didn't want to be one of them. I didn't want to be old and decrepit inside a cell because of something I didn't do."

In 1998, as he contemplated dropping his appeals, he got a visit from a lawyer named Denise LeBouef, who worked with the Capital Post Conviction Project of Louisiana. "She walked in there and convinced me that she didn't think I did it, and she wanted the opportunity to prove it," Thibodeaux says. "I told her I wasn't trusting of lawyers and she understood that."

Thibodeaux had little hope LeBouef would rescue him. But with nothing to lose, he became her client and saved himself from what would have effectively been suicide-by-passivity. That day marked the start of his slow ascent from rock bottom. The climb would take more than a decade.

Thibodeaux gets asked all the time how he did all those years in solitary confinement without going crazy. "I really have no answer," he says. "Call it a blessing. Call it a gift. Call it a fortunate eyes-open view of life."

Well, reading the Bible was a big part of it. He read it cover to cover four times, and still reads it today. "There are people all the time who tell me, 'There's no way I could have gone through what you went through.' But I would look at people like Job and David and the apostles and think there's no way I could possibly have gone through what they went through. That was a big help for me."

And knowing that good lawyers were working for him was paramount. After LeBouef signed on, so did Steve Kaplan from the Minneapolis civil law firm Fredrickson & Byron. "Their attitude was we know you're innocent and we're going to do our best to prove it," Thibodeaux says.

But more than anything, he stayed sane by adhering to a strict daily routine.

"I survived by repetition. Sometimes you get so bored, you don't know if you're going to lose your mind or not. So you just fall into your monotonous grind and let it envelop you."

A typical day started with brewing coffee using two quart-sized containers and a handkerchief as a filter. Then he'd get dressed, wash his face, brush his teeth, eat breakfast, and read his Bible. He'd wipe down his cell, make the bed, fold the laundry, go through some court papers, read the *Baton Rouge Advocate*, watch CNN, eat lunch, listen to some blues or country music on the radio, read a few chapters of a book (usually science fiction), do some push-ups, squats, jumping jacks, and sit ups ("anything to get you sweating and your pulse up"), take a shower, call his lawyers, have dinner, read some more, watch TV, do some more reading, get ready for bed, go to sleep.

Day after day after day.

The enemy was idleness—gaps in time when demons could get into his head. So he performed his tasks with a marine's determination. Some days, he used his hour outside the cell to run three miles up and down the tier. When the weather was good, he and other inmates would go outside into individual pens equipped with basketball hoops. They'd play a game where one at a time they'd shoot a basket. The first inmate who missed would have to do ten push-ups for every basket that was made before he missed.

Sometimes Thibodeaux made necklaces using silver and stone beads that he bought from a catalog. The beadwork was hypnotizing. "It gave me a way to just clear my mind and think about nothing but sticking the thread through the next bead, sticking the thread through the next bead, the next bead, the next bead."

Thibodeaux formed bonds with the men he shared the tier with. It did not matter to him who was innocent and who was guilty; everyone was in for murder, and all bore the same misfortune of having been convicted in a death penalty state. "It's crazy when you think about it," he says. "You have prisons where serial murderers get to serve life sentences and be with the rest of the population because they happen to be in a state that doesn't have the death sentence."

Death row inmates had an unspoken rule never to discuss their final destination. "We all knew why we were there. You just don't walk up to someone and ask, 'What do you think it will feel like when they stick the needle in you?'" When an inmate's time came, the others would watch silently as two officers escorted him down the tier in chains, never to return. They would never speak of it afterward.

Thibodeaux remembers Dobie Gillis Williams, who was thirty-eight when he died of lethal injection on January 8, 1999. He had been convicted fifteen years earlier of stabbing a woman named Sonja Knippers to death. "I was in the hallway at the time and he walked by with corrections officers, in chains and a jumpsuit, and he was gone," Thibodeaux says.

He did not mourn. "It's not an *I can't believe he's gone* type of thing," Thibodeaux says. "Everybody there is under the assumption that he and his neighbor is next in line."

Nor did Thibodeaux mourn the execution of Leslie Dale Martin, who was convicted of raping and murdering college student Christina Burgin in 1991. Martin took his final walk on May 10, 2002. He was thirty-five. "He was a down-to-earth guy," Thibodeaux says. "He was always either reading or typing on his typewriter. I valued him as a friend."

"I don't know if he did it or not," he adds. "That's between him and his maker."

Anyway, mulling over death is a waste of time when you're busy fighting for your life. Thibodeaux called his lawyers at least twice a week, and did legal research every day. Death row inmates did not have access to the law library, so they would put in requests to inmate counsels every morning for certain documents, and those requests would go to the law library officers.

The system was a pain in the ass.

"If they didn't think something you requested pertained to your case, then you wouldn't get it," Thibodeaux says. "Or, you'd get it, but it would be the wrong document. You wanted DNA stuff? They'd pick the first DNA case they came across, which was usually nothing more than a simple rape case. Well, that did me no good because mine was a murder case.

"The law says we're supposed to have access to the law library and we don't have access to the law library. If your request is governed by an administration whose job it is to kill you, they're not going to try to help you. They're going to try to put a roadblock in your path."

For a wrongful imprisonment case like Thibodeaux's that had so much proof of innocence, it took a prohibitively long time to get the proof through the right channels. Even after Jefferson Parish District Attorney Paul Connick joined forces with defense lawyers in 2007 to test the DNA evidence from the crime scene, it took another five years before Thibodeaux was finally released.

Despite the growing light at the end of the tunnel, those were not happy years. "You can't be happy on death row," Thibodeaux says. "To say someone is happy on death row is to say they're comfortable being there.

"I was sitting there day after day, waiting for them to just open the door and let me go. But the DA tested one piece of evidence at a time. I'm sure it would have been easier if he just sent everything together to the lab, but he's in control.

"So you keep your hope high but in the back of your mind you think maybe the DA is going to be a pain in the ass and say, 'No,' and you have to fight anyway. So I just kept joy in a bottle until I signed the log at the front gate at the prison in the parking lot."

The anticipation threw off Thibodeaux's rigid daily routine that had kept his delicate psyche at bay for all those years. "Everything that I put in place to help deal with the day-to-day issues of sitting in a cell all day become scrambled. I was trying to keep my repetitious mindset going, because if I let it deviate from my daily plan, things got thrown out of whack."

Not even the Bible comforted him. "What if my case falls through?" he'd suddenly ask himself in the middle of reading a verse. "Or if it doesn't fall through and I have to face the real world alone?" That last question gave Thibodeaux particular agita. It was becoming clear, as one DNA test after the next came back negative, that it stopped being an *if* and was now a *when*.

"What the hell am I going to do?" he asked his lawyer Steve Kaplan one day. "I have no job, no job history, no car. I'm going to have to pay rent, buy clothes, pay taxes. I have to learn to socialize with people again. Being in a cell for fifteen years, you're stripped of all that."

To take his client's mind off things, Kaplan sent him CDs and books—science fiction and historical works like an FDR biography and Doris Kearns Goodwin's Abraham Lincoln book, *Team of Rivals*. And he and Thibodeaux would discuss what he read.

The waiting went on and on as his lawyers slowly gathered evidence proving his innocence. They reached out to the two witnesses who'd claimed to see someone who looked like Thibodeaux standing near the murder scene. The witnesses now added a crucial detail to their story: they saw police tape at the scene. This meant they were there the night searchers *found* Crystal's body, not the night she was killed. And they had picked Thibodeaux out of a photo lineup only after seeing his image plastered all over TV. In short, they witnessed nothing of consequence.

The lawyers met with state pathologist Dr. Fraser MacKenzie, who had testified at Thibodeaux's trial. Now, MacKenzie heard for the first time that the details in Thibodeaux's confession did not match the physical evidence—namely, that here was no evidence of a rape. MacKenzie signed an affidavit for the attorneys pointing out the disparities in the confession.

MacKenzie also determined that Crystal died about two and a half hours after she left her home. Calculating the time Thibodeaux left the Champagnes' and the distance to the murder scene, it would have been virtually impossible for him to have enough time to commit the murder.

Most importantly, the DNA tests—which alone had taken two years—did not connect Thibodeaux to the crime.

On September 28, 2012, Judge Patrick McCabe, who'd presided over the original trial in 1997, ordered Thibodeaux be set free. He became the three-hundredth inmate freed by DNA evidence. That morning after breakfast, a lieutenant told Thibodeaux, "Pack your stuff, you're going home."

"I'm already packed," he replied.

But first there was one order of business that required Thibodeaux to don a jumpsuit and shackles one last time: a quick medical checkup. Until he walked out the door he was the property of the Louisiana Department of Public Safety and Corrections. When that was done, he changed back into a pair of blue jeans and a white T-shirt.

He picked up his bag and walked out of his cell and down the tier, unchained. He did not glance back.

"So long!" inmates called out. "Don't forget to be a voice for us."

At the front gate, Thibodeaux signed his name on a form. "No offense," he told the guards, "but I hope I never see you guys again."[4]

Then it was Thibodeaux and the open sky, reunited.

"It was kind of surreal," he says. "Here I am, looking at the sky not just as a free man, but one without chains on. It was almost euphoric; you know that feeling when you make a last payment on a car, or on anything that belongs to you that you paid for in installments? Multiply that a thousand times."

Steve Kaplan was waiting outside in a rental car. They set out on a three-day drive to Minnesota—Kaplan's home state—where Thibodeaux had decided to live because of the help the state gives exonerees. During the drive, Thibodeaux rolled down the window and stared for hours at the passing trees with leaves that were starting to turn brilliant reds and oranges. The air smelled wonderful.

That first night, they stayed at a hotel where Thibodeaux ordered a sirloin steak, well done, with asparagus and mashed potatoes. He ate it slowly, like he was tasting food for the first time. "It was probably the best meal ever," he says.

For the next five weeks, Thibodeaux stayed with Kaplan and his wife in Minneapolis. He nearly panicked in his eagerness to catch up on everything. "I wanted my car, I wanted my apartment, my job, I wanted it all at the same time," he says. "I had missed not having it for so long, here it was within my reach and I just thought, maybe I could fill that hole.

"I discovered I can't, no matter what I do."

Kaplan and his wife Pam told Thibodeaux to slow down and just enjoy having his life back. Sometimes he would just ride his bike to a lake and try to enjoy not being behind bars.

Then he'd get back to learning how to be a civilian. He practiced being around people again by taking walks through the Mall of America in Minneapolis and starting up conversations with strangers. He got a job doing clerical work in Kaplan's law office, and moved into his own apartment, provided by a St. Paul-based nonprofit called the Project for Pride in Living. He enrolled in a GED program and started taking computer classes. "Things had changed so much," he says. "We were using fax machines when I went to prison. The conveniences everyone has today weren't even a thought back then."

In prison, the beauty of Thibodeaux's daily routine was that there was no room for deviation. On the outside, there were so many *kinds* of routines, the choices were endless. "I didn't have to just get up, go to work, come home go to sleep. I could go out, have a beer with dinner, call some friends, go watch a movie, go for a drive. It's a bit of a task going from not just having life but actually living it."

For fifteen years, the only physical contact Thibodeaux had with another human being was the rare shaking of an inmate's hand. Even after deprivation dulled his sex drive, he still felt pangs sometimes for just a hug.

In May 2013, Thibodeaux went to a conference for exonerees in Georgia. He met a woman there named Veronica, who worked as an intern with the Witness to

Innocence nonprofit in Philadelphia. A month later, they
started dating. "With Veronica, when I get a hug or kiss
I don't get enough of it. I just want to soak it up, to savor
the contact." The couple plans to move to Austin in 2015
and get married.

Veronica, he is certain, is the one.

"She's intelligent; she's independent; she's kind, beautiful.
We share this comfortableness. We can sit next to each
other in the same room, not say anything to each other
all day long and be perfectly happy with each other. Or
we can have extended conversations about nothing and
still be happy with each other."

Thibodeaux is waiting on a wrongful imprisonment
suit against the state of Louisiana, but knows a payout
is cold comfort. "They can't begin to replace what they
took from me. It doesn't matter how big the judgment is
in the lawsuit. They can give me the world and still not
match what they took."

Of all the things they took, perhaps the most crucial
was the chance to be with his son.

When Thibodeaux was seventeen, he became a father.
And when Baby Josh was just a few months old, Thibodeaux broke up with his girlfriend and lost contact with
the boy.

Josh was fourteen and living in Alabama when he got a
letter that nearly knocked him over. It was from his father.
Thibodeaux introduced himself and said he'd fill in any
blanks that Josh wanted filled.

The boy wrote back, telling Thibodeaux about his life,
what he liked doing—hanging out with friends, playing
basketball and football. A lively letter correspondence
started. Thibodeaux drew the line at having his son visit
him in prison. "I didn't want him to see me in chains

for the first time. I didn't want our first meeting to be like that."

They finally met when Thibodeaux was free. "It was overwhelming. Here's my son, who I haven't seen since he was six months old, and now he's a grown man.

"And now he's a father, too."

Things are going pretty well for Damon Thibodeaux. He has a son and a girlfriend and a job he loves. He's grateful to the lawyers who set him free, and he's grateful for people like Bill Collins, from Interstate Truck Driving, who put him through truck driving school. "We exonerees have to eat, we have to pay bills, we have to pay taxes. We're just like everybody else now. And they don't make it easy for us to do that. It saddens me to see a lot of the guys who have been exonerated aren't as lucky as me."

Thibodeaux couldn't be happier hauling freight from one end of the country to the other. He knows what a daily grind feels like, and this is no grind. Because what always made him happy was a good view, and there's no better view than through the windshield of a big rig.

He chuckles at the irony of spending most of his hours as a free man inside an enclosure that's the size of a death row prison cell.

"This may be the size of a prison cell," he says. "But there's no bars in front of me. I can get out of the truck and go for a walk whenever I want.

"It's not confinement, and that makes all the difference in the world."

Chapter 2

JAMES KLUPPELBERG
Illinois, 24 Years

I've gone to hell.

That's what James Kluppelberg felt like walking through the gates of the maximum security Menard Correctional Center to serve out a life sentence for murder in 1988.

If prisons are fortresses of law and order, Menard was a quarantined ghetto—a graffiti-covered, drug-infested Wild West "administered" by a cowering warden. The real guys in charge were Chicago's deadliest gangsters.

Kluppelberg couldn't believe what he was witnessing.

Drug dealers hung out on corners wearing sweats, gold chains and baggy T-shirts—dyed blue for the Gangster Disciples, red for the Almighty Vice Lord Nation, gold for the Latin Kings. Glazed-eyed junkie inmates shopped around like old ladies in a fruit market, splurging on crack, cocaine, and marijuana at bargain-basement prices.

You had to look up high to see the corrections officers, perched safely in their watchtowers with shotguns in hand in case things got rowdy. But on the ground it was gang enforcers who patrolled the yards to dole out swift street justice. Wander into a rival's turf by accident? Automatic beat down. Get caught doing something really stupid, like snitching? Pray and beg all you want, it wouldn't matter.

You were going to get stabbed.

Kluppelberg watched in wonder as inmates in his gallery used their cells as personal crack dens, not even bothering to assign lookouts. Behind one set of bars an inmate weighed crystals on an electronic scale and bagged them. His next-door neighbor was strung out on the very same shit. A few doors down, a higher-ranking soldier was on the phone with his feet up, idly working out a crack delivery with the aplomb of someone ordering Chinese takeout.

The doors on the gallery weren't even locked.

"It was chaos. It was bedlam. It was just unbelievable," Kluppelberg says. "You would not imagine how wild Illinois penitentiaries were like back then. It would make the things you see on TV look tame."

Once, he saw an inmate get up from the table in the middle of a card game, pull out his knife and stab the other guy over and over because he thought he caught him cheating. "I just turned away and walked off the gallery," he says. "I didn't want to be questioned about anything."

Kluppelberg, who sat in prison for nearly a quarter century for a crime he did not commit, always walked away. And that's how he made it through the Illinois prisons without a scratch.

March 24, 1984, turned out to be the most important day of James Kluppelberg's life. He just didn't know it.

That was the day he joined dozens of his neighbors to watch firefighters battle a towering blaze that had consumed an entire apartment building and was threatening to spread. "I remember the massiveness of it," he says. "I remember it engulfed three buildings and did damage to a fourth and fifth. I remember the large amount of equipment and personnel. I remember a lot of people standing around. It's amazing how many people came out to watch."

Kluppelberg was nineteen at the time and living with his girlfriend, her young kids, and the kids' drug addict father in a house in the South Side of Chicago. The chaotic living arrangement had a lot to do with why he'd been so pissed a few hours before the fire.

Kluppelberg had come home to find the house a dump, with the kids unfed and everyone else giddy on coke. Enraged, he stormed out of the house to cool off. Then he came home and got in a screaming match with his girlfriend, Dawn Gramont. So he took a second walk.

When he wasn't mad anymore, he joined Dawn, her ex Duane Glassco, and Duane's girlfriend Michelle Briton for a card game. As they played they noticed police lights outside the window. Kluppelberg looked out to see what was going on. He saw a bright glow. The building on the other side of the block was burning ferociously.

It looked bad enough for Kluppelberg and Dawn to load the kids into the car in case they needed to flee. They also went to their landlord's house and woke him and his wife. Then they stood back and watched the building burn to a blackened shell. When the fire was finally out, the crowds dispersed and he and Dawn brought the kids back inside.

A few months later, the couple broke up and Kluppelberg moved out. The fire was already a distant memory. Kluppelberg didn't know until three and a half years later, when he was on the hook for murder, that it wasn't just a building that was destroyed. A family of seven, the Lupericos, had been sleeping in their second-floor apartment when the smoke woke up Elva, the twenty-eight-year-old mother. She roused her husband Santos, who quickly realized the flames were blocking the front and back doors.

So he told Elva that he'd go out the window and she could hand him the children. But before he made it to the window, he fell through the floor. Rescuers managed to get him to safety. They could not do the same for Elva and the children: Santos, Sonia, Christobel, Yadira, and Anabel.

The police Bomb and Arson Unit investigated the fire and could not find evidence of an accelerant. They ruled the fire an accident and closed the case.

Three and a half years went by.

In late 1987, Kluppelberg was married with kids of his own. He was trying to get a home remodeling business off the ground, and moonlighted as a security guard. Life overall was just fine.

During his security shift one night, he saw two parked cars that were on fire, so he called the cops. The incident wasn't so out of the ordinary in that neighborhood, and Kluppelberg forgot about it.

A month later, he was working on some pipes at an apartment building when police came by and said they wanted to show him some photos related to the car fires. They took him back to the Bomb and Arson squad office in downtown Chicago, where detectives sat him down in an interview room.

And they asked him why three years earlier he'd burned a mother and her five kids to death by setting a fire in their building.

If the cops hadn't looked so dead serious, he would have thought there was a punchline. "You mean the fire at South Hermitage Avenue?" he asked. He had barely given the incident a thought since it happened. He didn't even know anyone had died.

"That fire had no relevance to me," he says today. "I didn't know the people who lived in the building. I had no ties to the building in any way, shape, or form. It was just a fire in the neighborhood."

The detectives threw questions at Kluppelberg and he

started sweating. When he asked the police what they were doing, they slammed him against a wall and cuffed him.

Kluppelberg said he was innocent. The detectives called him a liar.

"Just tell us it was an accident," they said. "Accidents happen. We'll take care of it."

Things snowballed from there as the detectives became more and more persuasive, first with their words and then with their fists. It got to the point where screaming, "I didn't do it!" was not going to cut it. "For me, the turning point was when I started urinating blood. When blood starts exiting parts of your body it's not supposed to exit, it gets your attention really fast."

Kluppelberg could take no more. He confessed—to everything: the fire of 1984 and a host of other fires, including the burning cars that he'd reported to cops a month earlier.

The police charged Kluppelberg with six counts of murder and locked him up in Cook County Jail, where he'd stay for a year and a half. He showed up looking like he'd just lost a bout to Mike Tyson; there were two large bruises on his lower back. He pissed blood for a week.

"When you think about how, in the blink of an eye, I went from a husband and a father and someone who was just starting to get his life together to having it all ripped out by—" Kluppelberg stops mid-sentence. "That's a hard pill to swallow."

It wasn't until he got a copy of the prosecutor's discovery that he learned who he could thank for all this: Duane Glassco, his old housemate. Glassco had had some legal trouble of his own, including getting arrested the previous month for burglary, theft, and violation of probation. To get a break, he needed someone to snitch on.

So he told police he'd seen Kluppelberg start the fire that killed the Luperico family.

When Kluppelberg was a teenager he did some time in juvie for burglarizing a Radio Shack and a Currency Exchange. That experience did nothing to prepare him for the filth and violence of Cook County Jail, a rat's nest packed so tight with bodies that Kluppelberg often was forced to sleep in the floor of the dayroom.

But his faith in the justice system gave him comfort that eventually he'd come out of this nightmare. "I believed that when I finally did get a trial date, when I was finally able to tell my side of the story, I would be found not guilty," he says. "I believed that. Every morning I woke up, every time I went to court, I believed they would get it right."

Nine months in, Kluppelberg scored a legal victory: a judge tossed out his false confession after reviewing his claim that it had been beaten out of him. (He later learned that the cops who interrogated him worked under Commander Jon Burge, who would eventually do federal prison time for torturing suspects into confessing to crimes.)

But the judge did not throw out the charges.

When the trial began in 1989, the prosecution's key witness was Duane Glassco. He testified that hours before the fire, he and the two women in the house had been boozing and doing lines of angel dust when Kluppelberg showed up and got hostile. Kluppelberg argued with Dawn and then stormed out of the house.

That part was true.

This part wasn't: Glassco watched from the attic window as Kluppelberg made several trips across the backyard to the back door of the building where the Luperico family lived. On one trip, Kluppelberg hauled over a pile of newspapers. On another, a plastic bag he'd lifted from a pile of junk next to some trash cans.

Soon, Glassco smelled smoke.

Kluppelberg returned home, and the two young men stood at the attic window and watched the building across the way burn to the ground.

"Why did you do it?" Glassco said he asked Kluppelberg.

"You know how I am when I feel like I'm losing someone," Kluppelberg supposedly answered. "I do stupid things."[1]

The other key witness was Captain Francis Burns of the Chicago Fire Department, who testified that he'd gone to the fire, but only as part of a training exercise. He said he remembered the burn patterns indicated it was arson, though he admitted he had no notes to that effect.

Had Kluppelberg been wiser, he might have sensed the gravity of these two witnesses' testimony. But he simply thought Glassco and Burns sounded too ludicrous for anyone to take seriously. He remained confident that a not guilty verdict was imminent—especially since the most damning piece of evidence, his confession, never made it into trial.

On July 14, 1989, Judge Loretta Hall Morgan asked him to rise.

She said, "Guilty."

It couldn't be, but it was. Kluppelberg felt like he had just stepped into a Hanna-Barbera cartoon where the good guy gets frozen solid by the villain's ice ray. "I was just numb," he says. "I just sat there with a frozen look on my face. I couldn't move. I couldn't talk. I heard her saying it, but I just couldn't understand it. I just really couldn't."

Then came the second big surprise: the prosecution announced it was seeking the death penalty.

"Up until that point I didn't even know it was a death penalty case," he says. "That's how oblivious to the law I was. I didn't even know that I was fighting for my life. I just remember staring first at the judge, then at my attorney, then at my wife, thinking, *How could this be happening?*"

Later, he'd wonder if the guilty verdict had anything to do with his apparent lack of remorse for the deaths of that young mom and her five kids. But that's just the thing—he *felt* no remorse.

Because the fire happened three years earlier.

Because the human heart can't mourn for every child who dies a terrible death.

Because he didn't do it.

That night, Kluppelberg's wife Bonnie visited him in jail and they spoke through a dirty piece of glass smaller than a square foot. "We just stared at each other in disbelief, her crying, me crying, neither of us understanding it. I said we'd fight it; *somebody* would listen to us."

Kluppelberg spent eight months in jail awaiting sentencing, busing back and forth from court every few weeks to try and sway the judge to give him life instead of death. The redundancy of the stressful routine was broken by a bizarre incident in October 1989, that became a minor sensation in the local papers.

Kluppelberg's bond was inadvertently lowered from "no bond" to $25,000. His mother scraped together the 10 percent minimum in cash to pay the bondsman, and he walked out of jail. He got a rental car and started heading south until he was rearrested in Macon, Georgia.

The facts of how this came about are disputed. Police claimed Kluppelberg had bribed corrections officer Robert Velasquez to alter the record by arranging for Velasquez to receive $3,000 worth of cocaine from outside the jail. Kluppelberg says he doesn't know why his bond was lowered; he just went to court one day and was given the OK to post, so he did. He wanted to see his sister in Florida one last time, so he drove south. But when he heard authorities were looking for him, he phoned the Illinois State Attorney.

"I said, 'I'll be back for my court date. I'm out on bond,'" Kluppelberg says. "He requested I not travel any further, and tell them where I was." So that's what he did, and he called the sheriff in Macon, too. Before long, he was settled back in Cook County Jail, and that was the end of that.

Despite his devastating loss at trial, Kluppelberg says he was "very, very optimistic" that not only would he be spared the death penalty, but that Judge Morgan would overturn his conviction. That's because he got a new, better lawyer from the public defender's office who did his homework and discovered that Glassco could never have seen Kluppelberg walk into the back door of the ill-fated apartment building because there was another building blocking his view.

Kluppelberg filed a motion for a new trial based in part on this new evidence.

On March 22, 1990, Judge Morgan turned down the motion, saying Glassco had never claimed to have seen the *entire* apartment building. Never mind that Glassco's actual claim—that Kluppelberg had come and gone from the *back entrance* of the apartment building—had been disproven. Morgan sentenced Kluppelberg to six life terms in prison without parole.

However, she rejected the death penalty because of his youth and troubled childhood.

"In my eyes, being spared the death sentence meant that I was going to be able to fight," he says. "It meant that I would get out some day. It just took a much longer time than I thought it would."

Kluppelberg spent a month in the intake unit of Joliet Correctional Center, forty miles southwest of Chicago—the same prison John Belushi's Jake Blues gets discharged from in the opening scene of *The Blues Brothers*. The unit felt like a bus depot, as each day brought in another crew of convicts to replace those getting dispatched to assignments across the state.

It took less than a day for Kluppelberg to learn he'd truly left the civilized world behind. He was waiting in line at the chow hall when a melee broke out at the other end of the room. Then he heard it.

Click clack.

BOOM!

Kluppelberg hit the floor. The warning shot had come from high up in a tower, where the corrections officer wielding the shotgun was now surveying the room with a smug look on his face.

In time, shotgun blasts would become just part of the soundtrack to Kluppelberg's day. "Ninety percent of the time, that first shot would stop it. But if two people were fighting and one of them pulled a weapon and the warning shots didn't make him drop it, the officer would drop him in a heartbeat."

Kluppelberg got sent to Menard Correctional Center in southern Illinois. And though he spent more than a quarter century behind bars, it was those wild first six years at Menard that branded his experience.

Menard, which houses about 3,500 inmates, is nestled away in Chester, the hometown of "Popeye" creator Elzie Segar. The town takes great pride in that. When you drive along Chester's quaint streets, here and there you can spot statues of Wimpy, Olive Oyl, and the rest of the gang. But the tour stops abruptly when you get to Menard's brick walls.

Prior to the Illinois prison reform of 1996, gangs ran the state lockups. When Kluppelberg walked through the gates of Menard, he had the disorienting feeling of being led from bondage to freedom, not the other way around. Except freedom meant living in the world's most dangerous ghetto.

"It was like being in a little city," Kluppelberg says. "People were hanging around corners like they were in their own neighborhood on the South Side, doing whatever they wanted. It was amazing to see, it really was." Just like in the streets, the gangs had organized themselves into military-like hierarchies. There were foot soldiers, security officers, treasurers, yard enforcers. Up top were the leaders who brought thousands of dollars' worth of crack and cocaine into Menard every day.

Smuggling the drugs in was easy, especially when so many corrections officers were willing to be mules for a cut of the profits. Inmates' girlfriends and wives would help out, too, stashing drugs in their shoes, under their wigs, or even in condoms tucked into their nether regions. Some adventurous gangsters even arranged to have associates on the outside hit golf balls full of cocaine over the prison walls.

The upper echelon had every luxury in their cells—stereos, portable washers, VCRs. Underlings served them gourmet meals on trays, like butlers. Best of all, they had the keys to their cell doors and could come and go as they pleased, twenty-four hours a day, with their entourage.

Turf was so fiercely guarded that one could get stabbed just for using a pay phone designated for another gang. Violence was so common and delivered so arbitrarily that no one walked around without a knife strapped to his chest or tucked into his waistband. In fact, one could even get jabbed once or twice by his own enforcer as penalty for *not* carrying a blade.

Gang leaders did not tolerate insubordination, and this applied to inmates and officers. If a guard unwittingly offended a high-ranking gang member, word would get to the prison administration: move this guy to another unit or we'll kill him.

Prison brass, fearing for their own safety, ceded all sorts of administrative decisions to gang leaders in an effort to appease them. "It was so easy," Kluppelberg says. "Whoever was in charge of a gang would go to the administrator in charge of the cell house and say, 'So-and-so, who's living in Cell Five, is now living in Cell Seven, and this guy's gonna have a job here, OK?' And they would do whatever they were told."

There was nothing worse at Menard than being a neutron—someone who refused to enlist in a gang. That meant you were a subhuman marked for servitude at best and sex slavery at worst. Kluppelberg knew one neutron whose first cell assignment was with a member of the all-white gang the Northsiders. The poor guy spent his first week chained to the toilet, getting raped night after night.

Kluppelberg was fortunate to have a brother-in-law on the outside, a midlevel member of the Latin Kings, who had contacted pals at Menard ahead of Kluppelberg's arrival. The Kings welcomed him as a friend, which meant he could be neutral without being a neutron. All he had to do was keep his head down and stay out of trouble.

He wasn't foolish enough to go unarmed, though. He became an artisan in homemade knives. "You could turn the most mundane things into some of the nastiest, most treacherous weapons you'd ever seen," Kluppelberg says. "Take a deodorant container. Doesn't seem like it can do much damage, does it? Take that same container and take an open flame and you heat it to where it gets soft. You heat it and you stretch it, you heat it and you stretch it, you roll it and you keep working it. You've got a very nice six-to-eight-inch piece of plastic, and sharpen a point on, and you've got a very deadly weapon."

Kluppelberg neither drank nor did drugs, but there were other illegal pleasures on the market that he was privy to. Inmates ran takeout restaurants out of their cells, deep frying chicken in large metal cans swiped from food services, and baking pizza in ovens stolen from snack kiosks. They even grilled burgers on their bed frames, burning milk cartons underneath as fuel. The stuff was better than any fast food Kluppelberg had eaten on the outside. "If I wanted a cheeseburger or some fries or some fried chicken, I'd tell someone, 'Here's a couple bucks, go get me two pieces of chicken.' It was very good. It was either that or you were going to eat crap."

Personalizing your cell was another admittedly nice perk at Menard. Inmates painted their walls gang colors and tagged them with gang symbols, and even hung their own gang-color curtains made from terrycloth stolen from the prison's towel manufacturer.

Kluppelberg had nice brown curtains that he strung up to the shelving brackets above the door. He could draw them shut and enjoy going to the bathroom in privacy, or just kick back and watch TV and pretend to be in the comfort of his own living room. "It was definitely breaking the rules, but everybody did it so it wasn't *considered* breaking the rules. It's the same thing as when you're driving on the highway. If the speed limit's fifty-five but everybody's doing seventy, why do fifty-five?"

But fried chicken and terrycloth curtains were small beans compared to the most outlandish perk of all: the prison picnics.

Every year from April to October, each of the prison's clubs turned the rec yard into a full-on block party, complete with enormous tents, a barbeque pit, and women galore. Each inmate could invite four guests from the outside, so there would be hundreds munching on burgers and ribs, bumping and grinding to hip-hop, and "reuniting" with old flames: A girl wearing a skirt would sit in her boyfriend's lap. A couple would lean up against a table. Some couples were even less discreet, simply asking three or four guys to create a human wall in front of them so they could get busy.

Then one day in April 1996, everything changed.

Kluppelberg got up that morning, dressed and brushed his teeth, and waited for his cell door to open so he could go to breakfast. But it didn't open. Instead, a guard handed him breakfast through the bars. The same happened at lunch and dinner.

A lockdown. Common enough at Menard, usually after someone got killed.

But after a week without leaving his cell for so much as a shower, Kluppelberg knew something big was afoot—he just didn't know what. "It was torturous," he says. "What made it especially hard was the unknown."

Two weeks, three weeks, four. Still no word. His six-by-ten-foot cell seemed to shrink an inch or two every day. He and his cellie—short for cellmate—figured out how to shower by straddling the toilet and running water over themselves with a piece of tubing attached to the sink faucet. "And then what?" he says. "I did some research on my case, some legal work. The rest of it was just spent watching TV, playing cards, chess, dominoes. I was just trying to kill time."

Eventually, word reached the inmates that the corrections department was taking back the prisons, doing a cell-by-cell sweep to remove all weapons and narcotics.

There would be no weaning, no negotiations. Just an absolute, rip-the-bandage-off style of enforcement. When it was all over, the drug operations would be crippled beyond repair.

Kluppelberg had once done a six-month stint in solitary after his cellie fingered him for hiding homemade knives. The lockdown was much worse. At least in solitary he got his one hour outside every day. At least he could cross off the days on the calendar.

The lack of air conditioning made the lockdown even more unbearable. "It was brutal," he says. "The cells would get to 105 degrees on average without air movement. You'd try to sleep as much of the day away as you could to avoid moving around in the heat. A lot of the time you were up all night anyway, and it wasn't really much of a sleep. It was a semiconscious state in which you'd not only soak through the sheets but the mattress, too."

One morning in early June, two months into the lockdown, the sweep reached Kluppelberg's floor. He, his cellie, and eight others were shackled together and marched to the gym, where they were allowed to shoot hoops for a few hours.

In the afternoon, they came back to their cells. Each encountered a pile of his stuff on the floor and a stack of slips for every item the prison had confiscated. Anything not bought at the commissary had been seized, including items that had been ordered through approved catalogs—colored T-shirts, cable boards, extension cords that were any color other than white.

What hurt the most for Kluppelberg was losing the half-dozen ceramic Christmas figurines he had bought one by one since the beginning of the year. "When you make twenty-eight bucks a month and something costs ten bucks, it takes you a couple months to save up for something like that," he says. He'd been planning to mail them to his kids.

But he quickly forgot about those. "My cellie, he was hollering, yelling, and screaming, 'They took this from me! They took that from me!' But to me, those were just possessions. My goal, my crosshairs, my focus, was release. That's what I fixated on—to be released."

When the lockdown finally ended that November, Menard looked like a real prison again. Inmates wore identical uniforms sans jewelry or any gang markings. Those without work assignments had to stay in their cells for twenty-three hours a day. The curtains that once gave them privacy had been torn away.

Corrections officers who'd cowered when Menard was ruled by gangsters now developed what inmates called false courage. "They decided it was time to get even. Anything from shakedowns to the way they talked to you had an air of we're in charge now," Kluppelberg says. "Let's say you raised your voice while arguing a point. They would just put a pair of handcuffs on you and take you to segregation. If you so much as misstepped out of a column, they would put handcuffs on you and take you to segregation."

Now that homemade fried chicken and burgers were history, inmates were back to eating putrid chow-hall grub—usually some sort of ground turkey-and-soy mixture cooked into patties, sausages, or loaves. "When you got lunch meat, it was grey with a greenish tint to it because the chemicals in the food product reacted with the chemicals in the aluminum trays where they slice it. It was rancid and hard on the digestive system. Some soybean in your diet is good for you, but to the extent that they were giving it to us it was very hard to digest."

The only alternative to indigestion was going hungry, and that happened often enough anyway. Inmates could never predict exactly when the dinner bell would ring. If you were on the toilet and couldn't get out of your cell in time, the door slammed shut and you were out of luck. And if you told an officer, "Hey, I want to go eat," you'd get a ticket for disobeying a direct order.

Despite these setbacks, Kluppelberg found he preferred life post-reform. "It curbed a lot of the violence," he says. "Before '96, you had to be so careful. You couldn't go to certain parts of the yard because it belonged to this gang or that gang. You couldn't use this phone or that phone. There were all kinds of things you had to be conscious of.

"Now you didn't have to watch your back all the time."

"If there's one thing you learn in prison it's patience," Kluppelberg says. "The justice system moves incredibly slow—just astronomically slow—and you have to learn patience and humility. Those two personality traits really became a part of who I am now."

In 1998, Kluppelberg transferred back to Joliet. He later went to Stateville Correctional Center, and eventually returned to Menard. Those years were true purgatory, like waiting for the mailman who never comes—except when he does, he hands you another rejection to your appeal. Kluppelberg would shake off the disappointment and just get back to work. "I had so many lawyers and so many judges over the course of twenty-five years, it would boggle the mind of the average citizen."

He tried to make the best of the waiting time, enrolling in mail-order correspondence courses in religious studies. He earned an associate's degree in religious science and became an ordained minister.

He also watched plenty of TV on his thirteen-inch Zenith—time-killers like *The Big Bang Theory* and *Two and a Half Men*, and also plenty of educational shows like *This Old House* on PBS. He wanted to stay current on home remodeling so he'd be up to date when he got out of prison.

Meanwhile, Kluppelberg worked whatever jobs let him use his hands, like as a maintenance man and print shop mechanic. If those jobs weren't available, he took what he could get—snack vendor, law library clerk, data entry programmer, raw materials clerk for a mattress factory. Anything to stay outside his cell for eight hours a day.

As tough as it was getting those denial letters from the courts, a far more lasting pain stemmed from watching his family drift away from him. His wife Bonnie and kids Samantha and James Jr. vanished from his life, one by one.

"It basically was just time. Separation and time," he says. "I know that sounds like the short answer but that's what it was. There was just no contact, and the whole out of sight out of mind thing kicks in."

In 2000, he filed for divorce from Bonnie. "After a while, she basically got tired of waiting and she moved in with another guy. So one day I decided it was time for a divorce, to give her an opportunity to move on with her life." When the divorce was finalized, James Jr., who lived with Bonnie, stopped visiting. Kluppelberg would write to him and send him artwork, but never got a response back. It wasn't until years later that he found out James Jr. had stopped writing because he thought his father was a murderer.

"I understood why he could feel that way," he says. "He wasn't around when the fire happened. He believed in the system, just like most people do."

After splitting with Bonnie, Kluppelberg had a brief reunion with his first wife, Donna, whom he'd married, impregnated, and divorced when he was just a teenager. Donna and their daughter Samantha started visiting him regularly for a while. But when that reunion fizzled, Samantha vanished.

The one gleam of light was Sarah. Kluppelberg didn't know he'd fathered a third child, whose mother he dated only briefly, until Sarah wrote to him as a teenager wanting to get to know him. With that first letter, a thirteen-year correspondence was born.

Of all the family Kluppelberg lost while behind bars, the most painful was the permanent one. His mother died of stomach cancer on July 4, 2004. Kluppelberg didn't even know she was ill until the night before she died, when his sisters phoned from her deathbed. They put her on the phone. She said his name several times.

"Everything's going to be fine," she said, barely audible.

It devastated him to not be by his mother's side. "I didn't belong here. I was my mother's sole support before I got locked up. I took care of her; I took care of the whole family.

"She was mine, I was hers. It was crushing."

Ironically, the road to freedom started with another rejection letter, a denial on a post-conviction appeal that arrived at Kluppelberg's cell in April 2007.

His appellate lawyer mentioned she would put him in touch with a lawyer friend in the public defender's office who represented death penalty inmates. Since 2000, Illinois had put a hold on executions, and the state was on the verge of banning the death penalty altogether (that ban would pass in 2011). That gave the lawyers in that office a lot of time on their hands.

The friend agreed to meet Kluppelberg, and quickly

realized he was innocent and needed solid legal help. But her office would not take him on as a client because he was not a death penalty inmate. So she reached out to Jane Raley, a lawyer at the Center on Wrongful Convictions at Northwestern University. Raley sent two Northwestern law students, Ashley Schumacher and Cadence Mertz, to meet with Kluppelberg. After a few hours of talking, Schumacher and Mertz went back to Raley and said, "We need to help this guy."

Raley was just then taking on another inmate's case and didn't have time for Kluppelberg's. So she got a hold of Gayle Horn, a lawyer who ran the Exoneration Project at the University of Chicago Law School. In December 2007, Horn spoke to Kluppelberg on the phone and said she'd let him know soon if she, along with Schumacher and Mertz, would take on his case.

A few days later, he received a letter from the Exoneration Project. "I was shaking," he says. "I opened the letter. As I was reading it, I sunk to the floor."

"What, they turned you down?" his cellie asked.

Kluppelberg started to cry. "They're gonna help me."

Schumacher and Mertz threw themselves into the case, volunteering hundreds of hours of their time. Their subsequent bombshell investigation turned Kluppelberg's guilty verdict upside down.

Arson science had evolved a great deal since the 1980s. Francis Burns, the fire commander who had testified that the fatal fire had been deliberately set, had pointed to the shiny "alligatoring" patterns found on the building's remains as evidence that the fire had spread fast—as it would in an arson case. Twenty years later, the research now showed that they were fires that burned long and intensely, without an accelerant.

The lawyers also learned that police had had another suspect for the blaze, but never gave a report of her statement to Kluppelberg's defense attorney. Isabel Ramos had confessed that she might have lit up the apartment building after starting a fire in her own home nearby. But she was too drunk to remember.

Most significantly, the man who put Kluppelberg in prison recanted everything.

Duane Glassco signed an affidavit stating he never saw Kluppelberg go to the apartment building because another building blocked his view. Aerial photos confirmed as much. Glassco said he testified against Kluppelberg as part of a deal with authorities for a lesser sentence on various charges against him, which included burglary and theft.

He also did it because he was mad at Kluppelberg for dating his ex-girlfriend.

On May 30, 2012, Kluppelberg was doing some research in the Menard law library when an officer told him one of his attorneys was on the phone. He assumed this was a mistake. His lawyers were appearing in court on his behalf that day, and he always got the updates the day after court. If he took the call, he'd forfeit his monthly visit to the library.

"It's a mistake," he told the officer. "The call isn't supposed to happen until tomorrow." The officer walked away, and returned a short time later.

"Dude," he told Kluppelberg, "you've got to come now."

Kluppelberg was annoyed. He packed up his files and dropped them off at his cell. Then he waited in what was known as the bullpen for his counselor to escort him to the phone. When he finally picked up the receiver, he was put on hold while several of his attorneys joined in the conference call.

"Did you tell him yet?" someone asked when everyone was on the line.

"Will somebody tell me what the fuck's going on?" Kluppelberg said.

One of his lawyers, Karl Leonard, said, "It's over."

Great. I lost my appeal, Kluppelberg thought. "OK, so what do we do next?" he asked.

"We're coming to pick you up tomorrow," Leonard said.

Suddenly Kluppelberg understood. He dropped the phone.

It's over. He started shaking and tears rolled down his cheeks. *It's over.*

He picked up the phone and listened in shock as his lawyers explained that during that day's routine court hearing, the state had surprised everyone by dropping the charges.

Just like that.

The lawyers asked him what size clothes they should bring him. He didn't know; he hadn't bought a new outfit in a quarter century. "Don't worry about clothes," he told them. "I've got a new pair of sweatpants, a new T-shirt. Just come get me."

After hanging up the phone, Kluppelberg looked up to see wide smiles on the faces of his counselor and the officer in the room. "Couldn't have happened to a nicer guy," the officer said.

Kluppelberg was a quivering wreck. Life's possibilities, its joys and complications, were flooding his mind so fast he felt like he was drowning.

I have to get a temporary state ID right now, he thought. Otherwise he wouldn't be able to board the plane to Chicago the next day. *The plane!*

His birth certificate and other paperwork were in an envelope he'd hung on to for just such an occasion. He told his counselor he needed to get the documents and she accompanied him to his gallery, where the officer with the keys was eating lunch.

"Dude, I have to get into my cell," Kluppelberg said.

"I'm eating," the officer said.

"No, I need to get into my cell *now*."

"Can't it wait?" the officer asked.

"Dude, I'm going home in the morning, this woman's going to get me an ID, I need to get into the cell now."

The officer put down his fork. "OK, let's go," he said.

Once the ID was being processed, Kluppelberg sat on his bed for twenty minutes, trying to talk his heart rate down. Inmates and officers kept coming to his cell asking, "Is it real? Is it real?"

An officer asked if he wanted to eat in the chow hall. Kluppelberg declined, fearing an envious inmate might stab him. So the officer went down and grabbed him a couple trays of food, and followed up with an even nicer gesture by letting him shower alone for two hours, just standing under the hot water and clearing his head.

Back in his cell, Kluppelberg went through his belongings. Photographs, legal papers, personal correspondence, some clothes, and toiletries—that stuff he'd keep. Everything else he'd give away: stationery, fans, his typewriter, TV, radio, desk lamp, and about $150 of food. He'd even give his watch to an inmate who didn't have one.

He spent the rest of the night sitting in his cell, staring at the walls, waiting for dawn.

Kluppelberg was dressed, packed, and waiting at the door when they came to get him. It took four hours to process him, transporting his personal property to the front gate, getting him health clearance, turning in his state-issue clothing and bedding. He sat in the bullpen

of the administrative building while the office filled out
the last of the paperwork. They took his fingerprints one
last time.

With fourteen dollars in the pocket of his grey sweatpants, he met Karl Leonard at the gate. "It had been almost
a quarter century since I'd walked outside prison walls
without chains on. It was a very poignant moment. My life
had been given back to me and I just...it was very humbling."

What should have been an hour-long ride to the St.
Louis airport took four times as long because Kluppelberg was carsick and kept needing to throw up. The
airplane ride was far more enjoyable. A thunderstorm
delayed their landing for an hour, and as he looked out
his window at the storm clouds below, he thought about
where his life was just twenty-four hours earlier. This,
up in the air, was freedom. But what would happen after
he got off the plane? *Where will I live? How will I eat?*
he wondered.

"These are things that people don't think about when
they open the door for people like me and say, 'You can
go home now.'"

Kluppelberg's lawyers put him up at a Holiday Inn that
night and told him to get whatever he wanted to eat. He
went to the hotel bar and ordered a barbecue pulled pork
sandwich with fries and a Coke, a meal he describes as
"unbelievable." Then he went back to his room and dialed
a number with a New Mexico area code. The woman who
answered was named Rena Kilgore. They talked through
the night.

Kluppelberg had met Rena some twenty years earlier
when she'd written him with a question about the penal
system. She had been handling the estate of a dead friend
who had four sons, all in prison.

The two became pen pals and over time developed a relationship. Though Rena assumed he was guilty at first, she came to believe in his innocence. Eventually she trusted him enough to give him her number, just in case he ever needed it. One day, four years before Kluppelberg got out, Rena asked him, "Do you ever think about what if?"

That night at the Holiday Inn, Kluppelberg talked to Rena about what the future held for them. They decided she would visit him in Chicago in a week.

Kluppelberg needed a place to live. His lawyers were footing the hotel bill for a week, and then he was on his own. "I had literally nowhere to go," he says.

Meanwhile, James Jr. had seen his father on the news and reached out to Kluppelberg's lawyers. He'd long since stopped believing his father was a killer. A few years earlier, a lawyer and an investigator from the state's attorney's office had contacted him, asking if he'd implicate his father by claiming Kluppelberg had written him letters confessing to the crime. James Jr. said he wouldn't, because he had no such letters.

That got him wondering why, if his father was guilty, was the state trying so hard to keep him in prison? Maybe his father was innocent after all.

The day after he called his father's lawyers, James Jr. was at work when his cell phone rang. The voice on the other end was one he hadn't heard since he was a kid.

"Do you know who this is?" the man on the other end asked.

He and his father reunited that night at WGN-News studio in Chicago, where Kluppelberg was taping an interview about getting exonerated. They could barely hold their tears back, having not seen each other since James Jr. was a boy.

But practical needs kept emotions in check. They went to Kmart, where James Jr. bought his father some jeans and shirts, a watch, wallet, sunglasses, and other necessities. Then they went to dinner and ordered steaks and talked for the first time as father and son.

Early the next morning, the two drove to James Jr.'s house in Merrillville, Indiana, forty-five miles from Chicago, to meet his wife and daughters. Kluppelberg stayed for the weekend. On Monday morning, James Jr. asked his father if he'd like to move in with him for a while. Kluppelberg almost cried. "That would be great," he said.

"If it wasn't for my son asking me to come and move in with him and his family in Indiana, I don't know where I would have ended up at," Kluppelberg says now. "He was my anchor. Even though we hadn't spoken in over a decade, he didn't hesitate."

A month later, Kluppelberg took a trip to Fort Wayne, Indiana, to meet his daughter Sarah and her kids for the first time. "It was tense at first, because we had never met," he says. "She had been disappointed with people who'd come in and out of her life, who said they were going to be there and weren't." They went bowling, swimming, and went out to dinner. By the end of the weekend, they felt like family.

He has yet to reconnect with his daughter Samantha.

It was a whirlwind first few weeks, getting the barest of necessities of his life in order. The paralegals in Kluppelberg's lawyers' office gave him a crash course in modern technology—computers, email, cell phone usage. Then he set out to look for a job. And even for a man who learned the virtues of patience in prison, it was extremely tough going.

"It took me over a year to get a job," he says. "I put in

application after application after application and they would just ignore me."

He sent out nearly four hundred applications for anything from maintenance man to shelf stacker. In an already tough market, Kluppelberg had the added disadvantage of having no work history. When one googled him, the top of the search results showed that he'd spent nearly twenty-five years in prison for murder. "A lot of them didn't even understand what 'exonerated' meant," he says.

In one instance, he applied for a job as a maintenance worker for Kmart. As he was filling out paperwork at one of the company's warehouses, a supervisor asked, "Why is there this twenty-five-year gap in your work history?"

"Did you look at my resume?" he asked.

At the top of his resume, he'd written, AFTER HAVING HIS WRONGFUL CONVICTION OVERTURNED AT THE REQUEST OF THE STATE AND SPENDING OVER 24 YEARS IN PRISON UNJUSTLY, SKILLED AND AMBITIOUS WORKER SEEKS THE OPPORTUNITY TO JOIN A COMPANY AND CONTRIBUTE HIS SKILLS.

His lawyer Karl Leonard had even written a letter of recommendation explaining why Kluppelberg had gone to prison unjustly.

Kluppelberg handed a copy to the supervisor, who glanced at it and then excused herself for a few minutes. When she returned, she said, "I'm really sorry to have wasted your time, but we don't hire convicted murderers."

"But I've been exonerated," Kluppelberg said.

"But you were convicted," she said. "You were convicted as a murderer."

That was a low point. But persistence paid off, as eventually Kluppelberg found an employment agency that didn't care about his conviction. They got him a job in April 2013, at a steel tube manufacturing company. After a few months, he found an even better job as a maintenance coordinator for a senior building in Chicago. He replaces appliances, shovels snow, and fixes anything that breaks. "I love it," he says. "I'm very blessed to have been able to find a job that's similar to the one I had before I was incarcerated."

Kluppelberg eventually got his own place in Crown Point, a two-bedroom cottage that he shares with Rena. He's crazy about her; she's loving, generous, assertive, and down to earth. "She's very patient and understanding when it comes to me being way behind in the learning curve of life and socialization and everything else."

Like many modern American couples, their schedules don't jive. He works at the senior building from eight in the morning to four-thirty in the afternoon. She works the night shift as a dispatcher for a trucking company, from four to midnight.

But every morning at about two-thirty, he gets out of bed and talks to her for forty-five minutes. That's the one little stretch of the day they have together, and they make the most of it. On weekends, they catch up, go to movies and flea markets and sometimes just go out for a drive. "So far, we're making it work pretty good," Kluppelberg says.

On August 5, 2013, Judge Michael McHale granted Kluppelberg a certificate of innocence. "I find that a terrible injustice was done to Mr. Kluppelberg. I find it more likely than not that he did not start this fire," McHale wrote.

The certificate effectively erased the past. He could stop thinking of himself as an ex-con and all that comes with the label.

"A lot of people don't understand how important it was for me to actually obtain that certificate of innocence where that judge emphatically declared me innocent," he says.

Kluppelberg often gets asked why he isn't angry about what happened to him.

"For me to be mad or bitter would mean that I would have to dwell on what happened, and dwelling on it would give it continued power," he says. "I don't think it deserves that kind of power. It's taken so much from me. I just don't want to waste any more of my life."

Chapter 3

DEBRA BROWN
Utah, 18 Years

Debra Brown woke up one day in prison and felt a lump in her right breast. It didn't hurt so she ignored it. After a while she forgot it was even there, except when she wore a T-shirt and it protruded a little bit.

Five years after discovering the lump, on New Year's Eve 2001, Brown joined some other inmates in the rec room at Wasatch County Jail for Enrichment Night, during which ladies from the Church of Latter Day Saints would come and teach crafting and other skills.

That night, the LDS ladies taught the inmates about breast cancer. They set up three glass containers—one filled with white marshmallows, one with pink candies, and one with red hots—as a visual of the different stages of the disease. Brown stared at the containers and suddenly started trembling. She touched her lump and it felt like a chunk of rock. She began to cry.

"Being the farm girl that I was, of course I'd never put in to see a doctor because I wasn't worried about it, you know? It didn't hurt, and if it don't hurt, you don't go to the doctor's," Brown says.

The next day, Brown went to the Huntsman Cancer Institute in Salt Lake City, where a doctor took a biopsy.

On January 2, she took another trip to the institute.

An oncologist told her she had Stage 3 breast cancer.

Well, Brown thought, *I'm not going to have to grow old in prison after all.*

It had been more than six years since Brown had gone to prison for a murder she didn't commit. And at that point there really wasn't anything about her case that was positive.

But it wasn't her time to die. Doctors removed the lump, and few weeks later performed a radical mastectomy, which included wiping out the lymph nodes in her right arm. And to everyone's surprise, the nodes tested negative for cancer.

So Brown went back to being an inmate.

Immediately.

She was cuffed and shackled and loaded onto a van bound for the Utah State Prison in Draper, to recover in the infirmary there. As the officer put Brown's seatbelt on, he let the diagonal part slap against her chest, which was still draining fluid into a bag.

Brown shrieked in pain.

"Hey, sport," she told the officer, "just for your information, a mastectomy ain't between the legs; it's on the chest. Please don't do that again."

When Brown tells stories like this, she has a way of making them sound even sadder by laughing, as if to say, *Right? I can't believe it either.* She does it again telling this one: While she was recovering in the infirmary, the boiler broke and it got very cold. Brown asked an officer walking by if he could bring her some extra socks and another blanket.

"It's mind over matter," the officer told her.

"Yeah, well," Brown said, "I'm trying to imagine a fireplace, but it's just not working for me."

"No, you misunderstand me," the officer said. "*I* don't mind and *you* don't matter." He left the room.

Brown cried over that bit of cruelty on and off for days. *I* do *matter! I* do *matter!* She told herself over and over again. But it took a few weeks before she believed it.

She laughs again, and when she stops all traces of mirth in her voice are gone. "Those aren't the kinds of things you should go through by yourself," she says. "They don't give you a handbook and say, 'This is how you deal with it.' You either cowgirl up or you don't. It's that simple."

Debra Brown, a slender woman with pale blue eyes and wavy blond hair, gets her work ethic from her father, a bear of a man.

"Dad was the hardest-working person I've ever known," she says. "I'm not talking about eight-hour shifts; that was like a part-time hobby for him. I'm talking sixteen-to-eighteen-hour days, seven days a week, all his life."

After her parents split up, Brown and her older brother David would sometimes stay with their dad at his farm in Idaho. He'd rouse them early to pick corn, weed the fields, milk cows, and bail hay.

"If you're old enough to walk, you're old enough to work," he used to say.

"I remember there used to always be a big pile of scrap lumber, and if there was nothing else, we was to be out there pulling nails out of that—and not just pulling nails out of it, but straightening them out so they could be used again," Brown says.

Like her dad, Brown never quit working. When she was fourteen, she got her first job as a car hop at R&G's Drive-In in Smithfield. A year later she married a man ten years older and had her first son Ryan. By then she was working the production line at the Schreiber's Cheese factory in Logan and tending bar at night.

At twenty-one, Brown got divorced—not common practice in the predominantly LDS community where she
lived. Then she remarried and had two more kids, Josh
and Alana. She was pregnant with Alana when she filed
for her second divorce.

At the time, Brown worked at the snack counter of Smith's
Food and Drug in Logan, and money was tight. So she
felt lucky when one of her coffee regulars, a good-natured
older gentleman who owned a number of rental properties
in the area, offered her a job. His name was Lael Brown.
They were not related even though they shared a surname.

"Just a tall, lanky older fella who had a full head of hair,
but it was as white as white could be," she says. "He was
pretty wrinkled but I think that's because he smoked and
drank a six-pack of beer a night," she says.

Years later she'd be convicted of murdering that lanky
older fella, and would often think about that job offer as
what started it all. "I took on one job with him helping
him paint a house and one job turned into two and next
thing you know, I was working full time," she says. "That
man taught me how to paint, how to raise in a window,
how to sheetrock, how to texture, a little bit of plumbing.
He taught me everything."

Brown fell back on that job again and again for a decade
as she raised her three kids as a single mom. In the late
1980s she moved the family to Wyoming and then Mon-
tana to work in coal mines—and got married once more,
briefly. When she moved back to Utah, Lael and his rentals
were there waiting for her.

Lael and Brown met up for coffee every week, and
sometimes played hooky together to go trout fishing. "He
was just a good person. A good person," Brown says. "He
had a heart as big as a mountain. I saw him one time take

a string of pearls from this gal that was no more real than something you got from the five-and-dime but he took that as the deposit for an apartment because the gal was single with kids and just couldn't afford the deposit on it."

On Friday, November 5, 1993, Brown noticed Lael looked under the weather. One telltale sign something was off was he didn't order his usual slice of pie when they went out for coffee.

The next morning, Brown ladled some chicken soup with homemade noodles into a pan and drove it over to Lael's house in Logan. She knocked on the door but no one answered. She had a key and could have let herself in, but instead left the soup on the front steps with a note: *Made soup. Hope you feel better. Call if need anything.* Then she took her twelve-year-old son Josh to his middle school basketball game.

"You won't believe how bad that has haunted me," Brown says, referring the soup. "Everybody said, 'What about the soup? What about the soup?' Well, I thought Lael might be sleeping. And if he wasn't sleeping—well, Lael kind of was a chatty person, and I didn't want to be cornered all day."

After the game, she went to her boyfriend's house. They watched one of Brown's favorite movies, *Pure Country* starring George Strait, and then convened to the hot tub. Brown didn't get home until about three in the morning.

Later that Sunday she drove to Angie's Restaurant to meet Lael for coffee. But neither of his Dodge pickups was in the parking lot, so she drove to his one-bedroom house and saw both Dodges—the red one and the white one—parked outside. The chicken soup was where she'd left it on the front step.

Well, if you're that sick, I'm going to take you to the hospital, Brown thought. She knocked on the door a few times, but no one answered so she let herself in, using the house key Lael had given her.

The house was so small you could see most of the interior just standing at the front door. No one was in the kitchen or living room.

"Lael!" she shouted. No answer.

She turned left and walked into the bedroom.

Lael was in bed, facing away from Brown in a fetal position, with the blanket up to his shoulder. His head was resting in a puddle of blood the size of a large pillow. Brown touched Lael's shoulder. It was cool and stiff.

Lael's dead.

Brown ran screaming out of the house. Then she pulled herself together, went back inside and called 911. She was so shaken she couldn't remember Lael's address and had to find a piece of mail so she could read it to the dispatcher.

When police arrived, they found Brown sitting on the front steps, sobbing hysterically. They took her to the next-door neighbor's house. From there, she watched paramedics wheel Lael's sheet-covered body into an ambulance.

Later that day, two detectives stopped by Brown's home, asking if they could search the premises.

"What?" she asked. "Am I a suspect?"

The detectives promised her she was not. They said they believed Lael's death was a suicide, but had been unable to retrieve the gun. Had Brown taken it?

Taken the gun? Brown didn't realize until then that Lael had even been shot. She hadn't noticed any holes in his head—just the pool of blood. In her hysteria, she'd thought he'd died from a severe nosebleed. He used to get such bad nosebleeds he'd have to go to the hospital.

"We know that you're a friend of the family," one of the detectives said, "and if you've done something here, you need to tell us. Otherwise, you're interfering with our investigation." She assured them she had done nothing.

The next day, Brown got a knock on her door from a reporter and cameraman from KSL Channel 5. Their very presence riled her. She thought, *You vulture, all you want is a story. Don't you care I just lost my best friend?* But she politely told the men to wait at the door, and then called the detectives assigned to her case to see if she was allowed to do an interview.

The detectives said they couldn't deny her the right to do an interview, but they'd rather she didn't because it could interfere with their investigation.

Brown relayed the message to the reporter.

"Well no offense," he said, "but the Logan City Police Department couldn't find their ass if they had both hands to do it." He and his cameraman left.

Lael's funeral was that Friday. On Saturday, a detective asked Brown to come to the station and take a lie detector test. Police by then had determined that Lael's cause of death was not suicide but murder with a .22-caliber Colt Woodsman pistol. Lael owned such a gun, but it was missing along with his wallet, in which he used to carry thick wads of cash.

"Oh boy," she said. "I'm a suspect."

"No, Deb, you're not a suspect," the detective told her. "It's a process of elimination, and sometimes when we ask questions, you remember things that help us." She agreed to take the test, and did not think to bring a lawyer with her.

"I really thought I was part of a team to find the killer," Brown says now. "I'm believing this the whole time. I'm believing this."

The polygraph took about an hour. The examiner asked questions like, "Did you kill Lael? Do you know who did?"

"Of course not," Brown answered. She passed the test.

A month went by. Brown read the papers religiously for every scrap of information she could get about the case. And she had no contact with police, other than seeing an unmarked police car staking out her house every day.

One December morning, Brown was in her kitchen getting ready for work—her boyfriend, a roofer, had hired her as an assistant—when through the window she saw six squad cars with lights flashing swoop in all at once. The officers had a search warrant. They took her to the station for questioning.

This time they quit being nice. They demanded Brown tell them everything about her relationship with Lael and had her recount over and over every step she took the weekend Lael died.

And they asked her whether she killed Lael because she'd forged $3,600 worth of checks from his bank account.

"Forged checks?" Brown's face reddened. "I never forged a check in my life!"

That was her one lie, and she's mortified about it to this day. She was deep in debt when she started letting herself into Lael's house when he wasn't around to forge his checks. She wouldn't admit it to cops because she feared they'd pin it on her as a motive for killing Lael—which they did anyway.

"We know you owed Lael money," they said. "Did you guys argue? Is that was what this was about? Did you just feel trapped, like there was no way out?"

"No, no, no," she insisted through this interrogation and the many that followed. She kept denying it even after she went to prison, and it took years before she finally came clean to her family.

"I was so ashamed," she says. "There is not one excuse to breach a trust like that. I really sold everyone short."

Brown came back to a house that looked like it had been lifted off the ground and shaken. Investigators had ransacked her crawl space upstairs, ripping out the insulation and tracking it all over the house. They'd even pulled her Christmas tree out of its pot and dumped it on the floor.

The months that followed were a waking nightmare. Some twenty interrogations followed the first, and the forged checks were a constant thorn in her side.

Another growing problem was Brown's lack of an alibi for the period of time between six-thirty and ten a.m. the day she took the soup to Lael's house. That period fell within the thirty-hour span in which Lael had died, according to the medical examiner.

Her boyfriend, who had also been interrogated by police and whose house had been searched, stopped answering Brown's calls. Then one day he showed up at her door to apologize for disappearing on her, explaining that the detectives had told him she'd confessed.

"And you believed them?" Brown said. "If you believe I could do something like that, then get out of here."

The stress was getting to her. "It seemed like every corner I turned I'd see a property of Lael's that I'd worked on," she says. "I just felt like I wasn't gonna get past the trauma of what took place."

In March 1994, Brown took her two younger kids and moved to Hailey, Idaho, where she got a job as a baker at an IGA supermarket. At night she drove a taxi that shuttled people from Hailey to the resort town Sun Valley. She did that for six months.

On Friday, September 9, Brown drove the kids back to Logan to celebrate their birthdays. She'd booked them a poolside room at the Baugh Motel, and planned to cap the weekend off riding rollercoasters at Lagoon amusement park in Farmington.

Brown dropped the kids at their father's house, and drove to the motel to decorate the room with Mylar balloons and a three-layer lemon cake with cream cheese frosting that she'd baked herself. *Happy Birthday, Kids!* she'd scrawled on top with piping gel.

The motel desk clerk gave her the room key and she pulled the car around back. As she unlocked the trunk to remove the cake, a rather good-looking man approached her.

"You remember me, Deb?" he asked.

"No, I don't," Brown said. "Should I?"

"Yes, you should." He said he was the first police officer at the scene after Brown found Lael's body.

"Oh," she said. "How are you?"

"Better than you. I've got a warrant here for your arrest."

For about two seconds, Brown had the absurd thought that she was being pranked, and wondered where the camera was. Then, she says, "I was cuffed up, arrested, and never breathed another day of freedom."

Brown was charged with murder punishable by death.

But even after trading in her Wranglers and T-shirt for navy blue scrubs at the Cache County Jail, she still did not believe a conviction was possible.

Bail was set at $200,000. Brown's family wanted to put all their properties up as collateral, but Brown told them to hold off. "Forget about it," she told them. "I didn't do anything. I'll sit this out. There's no way I'm ever gonna get convicted."

Brown sat it out for thirteen months. A workaholic with no work to do, the idleness nearly drove her mad.

"I'd have gave anything just to get out of my cell, just to scrub walls or anything."

So Brown whiled away the days on her cot, reading humor books and eating licorice and candy bars. Her weight skyrocketed from 120 pounds to 178. When her trial got underway in October, 1995, she had to borrow a dress from a Bible studies teacher because she didn't own anything that fit.

The $3,600 in forged checks was the centerpiece of the prosecutors' case during the five-day trial at the Box Elder Courthouse in Brigham City. Prosecutors claimed Lael had discovered the forgeries and had confronted Brown, so she killed him. One by one, the fake checks were blown up on a screen for the jury to examine.

Almost as damning was Brown's inability to prove she was not at Lael's house when he died. By the time of trial, the medical examiner had narrowed down a much more exact time of death for Lael: seven a.m. on November 6. That fell within the three-and-a-half-hour period for which Brown could not provide an alibi. Prosecutors produced a female witness who testified she heard gunshots at about that time.

Brown's best witness was Lael's next-door-neighbor Gary Ogilvy, a bishop and retired cop who said he was up that morning and heard no gunshots.

Brown was scheduled to be the last witness for the final day of testimony. But before she took the stand, court broke for a recess and her lawyers took her into a small conference room.

"Deb," said her lawyer John Cayne, "I can't tell you not to testify, but it's in your better interest if you don't." He explained that the overwhelmingly LDS jury, with its high moral standards, might be put off hearing an accused killer—and three-time divorcée—speak, particularly if her story involved hot-tubbing with her boyfriend hours before she discovered Lael's body.

Brown had a moment alone in the conference room to think it over. She looked out the window and saw two white doves perched on the ledge—a good omen, she thought. She took Cayne's advice and declined to testify. The jury left the courtroom to deliberate, and Brown was transported to a holding cell. Prosecutors had announced by then that they were no longer seeking the death penalty, but life imprisonment instead. Perhaps, Brown hoped, a sign that their case was weaker than they'd let on.

As she waited in the cell, a bailiff having pizza offered her a slice. A transportation officer from the jail told him, "Oh, she's going home and eating with her family in a little bit."

After five hours of deliberations, it was time.

Officers led Brown back into the courtroom. The jurors filed back to their seats.

"How do you find the defendant?" Judge Gordon Lowe asked.

"Guilty," the foreman said.

Brown's grandmother gasped loudly.

Brown's voice trembles talking about what that moment was like. "It's like everything goes fuzzy. You can't believe what your ears are telling you. The unthinkable. The unimaginable. The thing you knew just was not gonna happen happened, and there wasn't a thing I could do about it."

Too bad prosecutors dropped the death penalty, Brown thought.

Officers cuffed her and as they led her out of the courtroom, she asked loudly, as if drunk, "What about the doves?"

The jail put Brown on suicide watch for a week. She lived in a glass-walled pod that was constantly monitored by an officer, with no privacy even to use the toilet. "What little dignity you might have left, you no longer have," she says.

"You just sit there and hope you'll pass away in the night."

Two months later Brown was hauled back to court and sentenced to life in Utah State Prison with the possibility of parole. Her stomach clenched. "You see movies about prison and hear about things that happen there. I wasn't this big bad person that they were locking up and throwing the key away. I was just Deb Brown."

Brown had gained so much weight in jail that when she tried to pull up her Wranglers for the drive to prison, they didn't reach her waist. So she just wore her jailhouse scrubs and got in the backseat of a Cache County squad car for the two-hour drive to Draper, home of Utah State Prison.

Staring out the window, she took in the picture-postcard views of the snow-capped Wasatch Mountains. Brown had seen those gorgeous vistas nearly every day she'd lived in Utah, and now tried to take mental snapshots. The deputy asked what kind of music she liked and she said country, so he put that on. "You'll be alright," the deputy said. "You'll be alright." But Brown was barely listening.

She was praying for a car wreck.

That afternoon, they pulled into a vast complex of beige brick buildings and watch towers, surrounded by what looked like miles of razor wire.

The four-thousand-inmate compound commonly referred to as "Draper" is about twenty miles south of Salt Lake City. It once housed serial killer Ted Bundy before he was extradited to Colorado for murders he committed there. It was also once home to Gary Gilmore, who made headlines when he demanded a speedy execution by firing squad for a double murder he committed in 1976. The state granted his wish in January, 1977.

Brown's heart pounded as the squad car passed through a series of gates before pulling up to the intake unit, where Brown showered and was ordered to don a prison-issue bra, underwear, and a set of maroon scrubs. A physician's assistant inspected her and an officer gave her a toiletry kit and a handbook of prison rules and regulations.

Officers escorted her to her first cell where she met her first cellie, a weathered-looking pill addict in her mid-forties named Ruby Petters. The veteran jailbird gave Brown tips on getting by in lockup. One thing she forgot to mention was how not to piss off other inmates.

The next day Brown unthinkingly walked in front of a TV that a bunch of women were watching. A hotheaded inmate from Polynesia jumped up and rushed her, grabbing her shoulders and shoving her back, bellowing curse words so foul that Brown is ashamed to repeat them.

Ruby broke up the fight and explained to the Polynesian that the newbie didn't know any better. Brown went back to her cell, put her face in her hands and sobbed.

After ninety days, Brown got to leave the intake unit and join the general prison population. And for the first time in a year and a half, she had a job—dishing out ladles of mashed potatoes and mixed vegetables for thousands of inmates. The work wasn't all that different than what she'd done in the past on assembly lines. It felt good to be put to use. When she wasn't working, she was either crocheting or taking Bible courses—Catholic, Mormon, Baptist, it didn't matter. She found serenity in the chapel, hearing the calming voices of the Bible teachers as they taught Scripture.

One day she got a visit from Alana and Josh, who by then were in their early teens. She had not had physical contact with her children since the weekend that was supposed to be their birthday celebration.

She wished she and the kids could be in a bubble, cut off from those inmates who gawked at them and from officers patrolling the visitation room making sure everyone's hands stayed above table level.

After an hour, the visit was up. It felt like ten minutes.

"You were *feeling* a little bit for a minute, and daring to dream. And then you have to see them walk out of there and you've got to go the other way," Brown says.

She went back to her cell and relived every moment of the visit, thinking about things she wished she had said. "You're just starting to numb up to being in prison and then you get to be around these precious ones that you love so much, so when they leave you hit bottom again.

"You just have to wonder if it was even worth it."

She cried every day for two weeks after that visit. And then the tears stopped and the numbness returned.

Just a few months after Brown arrived at Draper, the corrections department transferred her to the Wasatch County Jail in Heber City, just east on the other side of the Wasatch Mountains, to work as a cook there.

Brown was impressed when she arrived; Heber was a brand new facility with only 140 inmates, mostly transfers from overcrowded Draper. The yard afforded spectacular views of mountains and farmland, whereas the only view she got at Draper was of a cement wall.

And if Draper's food tasted like, well, prison food, Heber's was like something out of Julia Child's kitchen. Brown herself baked homemade bread, cinnamon rolls, lemon bars, and brownies. "It kind of became a calling," she says. "I lived in a little bubble world, where I'm on a mission here; I'm gonna feed these people. I sort of made a deal with God: if you take care of my kids and see to their needs, I'll take care of these kids in here that don't have access to their parents."

The county sheriff was enlisting inmates to crochet blankets and clothing for impoverished children overseas, and Brown was happy to join the ranks. "It felt pretty darned good to crochet a blanket or booties. We went through boxes and boxes and boxes of yarn. That was probably one of the best things the sheriff could have done for us."

The work was cathartic. Brown had had a lot of anger, and she felt it melting away. "When I went to prison, I hated the officers just because they had a uniform on; that was reason enough for me. Yet they done nothing to me. It was just the simple fact that I was blaming somebody. I was getting ready for work one morning when I realized I didn't know who I was anymore. I'd become so cold and so hateful. And I decided that day I was going to make some changes, try to become a better person."

In February 2002, Brown got her first and last visit from her father. He'd been diagnosed with lung and breast cancer three years earlier. "I know my dad; he just don't make trips like that. I knew he had to be getting close or he wouldn't have come."

Brown had trouble masking her horror at how much the cancer had ravaged her father's body. "I'd never seen my dad in my entire life not wearing cowboy boots, and that day he had on these big tennis shoes, and I remember his feet looking so huge and the rest of his body looking so gaunt. He went from being the size of John Wayne to about 118 pounds, and his skin was hanging, sagging."

The changes weren't just physical. Clark Scott had been stoic and callous for as long as Brown knew him, but now he seemed uncharacteristically sentimental and affectionate. It almost made her uncomfortable.

When they hugged good-bye, Brown was crying. She said she hoped they'd see each other again someday, knowing

full well that they wouldn't. Brown by then had been diagnosed with Stage 3 cancer herself and was awaiting her
mastectomy. It didn't look like either of them would make
it to Christmas.

"Take care, toots. Keep your chin up," Scott said.

He died at age sixty-two, on the first anniversary of
September 11. "That's dad for you," Brown says. "He would
have wanted to make sure we remembered the day."

As terrible as 2002 was for Brown, it was also the year
one of her Bible studies teachers, Vickie Rylie, heard her
story and became convinced she was innocent. Rylie wrote
to the Rocky Mountain Innocence Center in Salt Lake
City. Attorney Jensie Anderson, the center's president,
researched the case with a student and decided it was
worth looking into. "I didn't think Jensie stood a hope or
a prayer," Brown says. "How on earth was she gonna do
this? There was no DNA evidence to clear me. There was
nothing ever gathered. But just knowing that there was
someone out there working on it that believed me made
a world of difference in my whole attitude."

By 2004, Brown was back at Utah State Prison in Draper,
with no evident progress on her case. "I kind of lived
life much as I imagine an alcoholic does, still kind of
a numbed up state where you didn't dare to dream or
hope for anything because you didn't want to get your
heart broke."

Cellmates came and went so fast—most were in for
small infractions—that she rarely bothered to even speak
to them. She believes that over the entirety of her incarceration she had about 200 cellies, most of whose faces
she can't remember.

But there were two she remembers well, only because
they both made passes at her, both so awkwardly that she

is too embarrassed to get into details. All she'll say about it is, "I had to be real firm and clear that that was of no interest. And while it might be nice to get a massage, it kind of creeped me out. I didn't want to be touched. That was that."

There were other awkward moments. Once, Brown opened the kitchen spice closet to get some garlic powder and found an inmate pleasuring a male officer. Brown was too stunned to speak.

"You didn't see anything, right?" the officer asked her later.

"Yes, sir," Brown said, "You're absolutely right, I didn't see anything."

The prison chapel made her feel safe after such encounters. She was raised without religion, but the LDS teachers taught her about things that gave her comfort—"Uplifting, good things. Not dark things," she says—like the Mormon ritual of sealing, which keeps families together for eternity. "Of course you're gonna lunge towards that when you've lost so much time with them."

In 2008, things started looking up in Brown's case. The Utah State Legislature passed a law permitting convicts to present new evidence to the court proving that they are "factually innocent." Brown's lawyers filed a petition for such a hearing and got to work putting their findings together.

"Even Jensie was very cautious," Brown says. "She would say, 'I'm cautiously optimistic,' because she didn't want to get my hopes up." But Anderson kept Brown in the loop all the time, even if nothing was going on.

That same year, Brown and two other women applied for a sixty-by-sixty-foot gardening space in the prison yard. The warden gave the OK and inmates started planting vegetable seeds donated by Brown's brother David, who had a farm in Idaho.

"In about four weeks, you could see the things sprouting

out of the ground—the corn, the carrots, the onions, the radishes," Brown says.

Then something terrible happened. A pair of scissors went missing from a classroom, and the whole prison went into lockdown as officers searched for them. Brown watched from her cell window as a squad of officers went out into the garden with shovels and hoes. "And I mean they trashed it. They were high-fiving each other out there, totally enjoying themselves and laughing and having a good old time. Here we were doing something good and productive and it didn't cost them anything. I couldn't believe they were behaving like that."

There was no harvest that year. But the next year, the inmates grew a massive haul of vegetables that fed hundreds of prisoners. It was a shame Brown couldn't eat most of what she grew—at least not raw—because she wore ill-fitting dentures that the prison wouldn't pay to fix. Instead she ate mainly soft starchy foods like rice and mashed potatoes. Though the meat served at Draper was soft enough for Brown to chew, she wouldn't touch it. "We called the turkey 'skin graft' because that's what the slices looked like," she says. "It fell apart because it's was so watery. After slicing it so many times in the kitchen, I couldn't bring myself to eat it."

Meanwhile, the investigation into Brown's case was picking up steam.

Her lawyers had found two witnesses who said they saw Lael alive hours after the seven a.m. time of death determined by the medical examiner. One of the witnesses, Delwin Hall, said he'd even told prosecutors that he'd seen Lael at Angie's Restaurant that afternoon.

Hall had been on Brown's witness list, but had never been called to testify.

They found a man named Sylvan Bassett who told them about his pal Bobby Sheen, one of Lael's tenants, who got evicted for not paying rent. Bassett said Sheen owned a Colt Woodsman pistol—the same type of gun used to kill Lael—and had acquired a large amount of cash after the murder. Sheen had told Bassett he'd thrown the gun into a lake. According to Bassett, when he told all of this to police, they replied that if he "knew what was good for him," he would "let it go, leave it alone."[1] Sheen committed suicide in 2007.

The lawyers also re-interviewed a witness who testified at Brown's trial that she heard the gunshots at around seven a.m. Saturday—supporting the medical examiner's time of death. Now the witness was saying that she may have heard the shots on Sunday.

All of this was spectacular evidence. And if it hadn't been for that damned refrigerator, Brown would probably have gotten out of prison a year earlier than she did.

The weird-but-true incident happened like this: Brown's daughter and son-in-law answered an ad for a refrigerator a few blocks from where they lived in Logan. They showed up not knowing that the seller, Kevin Allen, happened to be the First District Judge of Cache County who was to preside over Brown's factual innocence hearing in 2010. Before hauling off the fridge, Alana and her husband were making small talk with the judge. Suddenly he frowned.

"You're Deb Brown's daughter," he said.

"Yeah," Alana said.

"Oh no," he said.

All it would take would be someone seeing Debra Brown's daughter's car in his driveway to put them all in deep water. He recused himself from the case, handing it off to another judge, for whom it took a year to get up to speed.

"A year is not that long," was the remarkably calm response Brown gave her lawyers when they told her about the shocking setback.

And so another year passed. Brown would sometimes walk into the yard and watch the three giant American flags on the other side of Interstate 15 billow in the wind. "I'd play this game with my mind," she says. "Look how the wind's blowing. It's blowing right in your direction and they're waving for you. For you, Deb, for you. Just hang tough."

In January 2011, Brown's lawyers went before Weber County District Court Judge Michael DiReda in the first hearing of its kind, and presented their new evidence pointing to Brown's innocence. One of the lawyers, Alan Sullivan, said their findings not only proved his client's innocence, but "placed in question the integrity of the entire investigation."

On May 2, 2011, Judge DiReda ruled that Brown was factually innocent.

A week later, Brown was up at four a.m. watching *I Love Lucy* on her cellie's TV when she saw a headline on the news ticker at the bottom of the screen that nearly made her levitate from her mattress. It said Debra Brown was to be released from prison.

At noon, she was ordered over the intercom to go to officer's window with her stuff—most of which she'd already given away. Officers drove her to the warden's office on the other side of Interstate 15 and locked her up in shackles in a small room.

Then, at one minute past two, they unshackled her. Alan Sullivan appeared and drove her to the prison parking lot. Clutching a clear plastic bag containing some books and photos, she opened the door and took her first step as a free woman. Rain was coming down in torrents, and it felt like the best shower ever.

At least one hundred people with umbrellas were there to greet her—family, friends, Bible teachers, lawyers, and a slew of reporters and cameramen. A church volunteer from Heber had laid out a red carpet, and Brown walked the length of it feeling like a Hollywood starlet—no matter that she was wearing baggy grey sweats made baggier by the rain.

She was free.

"Just being able to look around at those beautiful mountains without it being a distorted view, without looking through razor wire, it's a whole clear picture," Brown says. "And you're not sporting any shackles or handcuffs and you're able to hug as many people you want for as long as you want. I didn't care what I looked like. It just didn't matter."

Brown went straight from prison to Salt Lake City, where her lawyers had a pizza party for her in their office. The pizza smelled great, but she couldn't eat it because of her ill-fitting dentures. One of the staff ran out and got her oatmeal.

During the party, Utah's Attorney General announced on Twitter that he would not appeal the court's decision to free Brown. Jensie Anderson called the Attorney General's office to confirm the news, and once she got it, announced it to the room. Everyone broke into wild applause.

After the party, Brown's son Josh took her to meet his family in Brigham City. Then he drove her to a gas station where her brother David would take her to his home in Idaho to recuperate.

David filled up his tank before they left.

"You didn't pay for that gas," Brown said as they drove away.

"That's alright," David said. "The state owes us that."

That set Brown off in a panic. "David," she said tensely, "I am not going down for this. Turn this truck around."

David started laughing. He explained he *had* paid for the gas—with his credit card, before even filling up. He couldn't resist messing with her. That was the first of many surprises coming her way.

When Brown got to her brother's house that night, she opened the dozens of congratulations cards people had given her. And many of them had cash—about $300 altogether. Brown felt like she'd won the lottery. "It didn't look real," she says. "It looked like Monopoly money."

From there, it was one marvel after the next: she took a shower where she could control the water temperature, and walked barefoot on carpet so exquisitely soft it reminded her of cotton candy. The bed was so comfortable that she couldn't fall asleep, so she slept on the floor instead.

The next day Brown and her sister-in-law got ready for a family picnic. They went to a supermarket to buy some cheese, deli meat, potato chips, and baked beans. Brown had planned on paying with some of the cash she'd been given. "I almost passed out when they rang me up," she says. "I was thinking it would be something along the lines of twenty dollars. It came out sixty-some-odd dollars—for something we could carry out in three bags!

"I thought, oh man, I'm gonna starve to death. You go from making a quarter an hour to spending that kind of money. I'd just spent what would have been my whole month's check."

The first couple of weeks as a free woman were sublime. Nearly every day Brown would get up early and cycle on country roads so flat it was like riding on the ocean. David had bought her a light-blue bike while she was in prison, one she'd clipped a picture of from a magazine and mailed to her brother with a note saying, "That will never happen."

Two weeks after she was freed, Brown and her lawyers got some devastating news: the Attorney General's office had changed its mind and filed an appeal with the Utah Supreme Court challenging Brown's exoneration.

"That felt like getting slugged in the gut," Brown says. "I didn't know if I needed to run away and hide somewhere, or what."

Attorney General Mark Shurtleff told reporters that the evidence Brown's lawyers had presented was dubious, and that the judge's ruling made it too easy for prisoners to bring back questionable evidence that might persuade a judge to overturn a conviction. "We fear a floodgate opened [by the judge's ruling, and that every judge will be] giving another bite of the apple to everyone convicted of a crime," Shurtleff said.[2]

If the Attorney General won his appeal, Brown would not get compensated the half-million dollars the state owed her, and she might even go back to prison. She was terrified. But all she could do was wait for the court's slow gears to turn.

Meanwhile, she got her first job, working at the deli counter at Lee's Marketplace in Smithfield. She quickly rose to become night shift supervisor. After finishing her shift one morning, Brown left the store and saw the word "Killer" written in snow on the rear windshield of her car. Not long after, someone busted her front windshield and left six .22 shell casings on the hood—the same caliber used to kill Lael. She called the police, but they did little to investigate.

"I went into a world of panic," Brown says. She started driving her uncle's truck and parking it in the store's loading area where the security cameras were. Then one day as she was driving home she noticed a car following her. The car kept going after she pulled into her aunt and uncle's driveway, but she'd had enough.

"I decided that was it," she says. "I looked at those customers and wondered, is it her? Is it him? I worked my last shift and told them I wasn't coming back." Brown packed up and moved 570 miles away to Ahsahka, Idaho, to work at a bed and breakfast. There, she felt safe.

On July 14, 2013, the Utah Supreme Court upheld Judge DiReda's factual innocence ruling. Brown was officially exonerated and eligible for more than $500,000 in compensation. She was picking blackberries by the Clearwater River in Idaho when she got the news.

Lawyer Jensie Anderson told a reporter that day, "I've known Debra Brown for twenty years and I've never heard her laugh with that kind of joy and that kind of relief. It was music to the ears."

In October 2013, Brown got her first payout of $114,000, with payments of $44,000 to follow each year for the next nine years. Though this is more money than she's ever possessed, she still has to work to make a living. She had no 401K in prison and figures she has ten to fifteen good years to get some kind of retirement plan built up.

And, she says, "I would so give every penny I make working, plus what they gave me, to have those seventeen years back and my family back."

After moving from job to job, Brown may have landed the perfect one. In the summer of 2014, she bought a restaurant in Ahsahka called the North Fork Cafe, which sits right where the North Fork River meets the Clearwater River. The cafe is popular with fishermen and deer hunters, and is locally famous for a half-pound burger called the Lumberjack.

Brown waitresses, bakes pies, and prepares all the sauces, gravies, and soups. She works from dawn to dusk, seven days a week, and loves every minute of it. "Business has just been crazy," she says. "When I was in prison and polishing my skills in the kitchen, I thought about how cool it would be to have my own place."

Workplaces have always been like second homes to Brown, be they bars, coal mines, deli counters, gas stations, ice cream factories, or cafes. Sometimes Brown wonders if her love affair with work got in the way of raising her kids. "I worked two, three jobs at once instead of giving those kids what they really needed, which was me. I was trying to give them material things. I didn't want them going without things because of choices I made to be single. As it turned out not only did they not have a dad, they didn't have a mom either. But they had nice clothes."

Brown treads lightly when speaking about her kids. They are devout Mormons and she is not. But religious differences may play less of a role in the state of their relationship today than the fact that the kids were children when their mother disappeared, and adults when she came back. By then, she was a grandmother of nine.

In prison, Brown would dream of her kids running into her arms as they once had, the grandchildren clinging to her Wranglers every time Gramma came for a visit.

That is not how it has been.

One Sunday, Brown went to a dance performance for Alana's daughters, not knowing she was supposed to bring flowers. It wasn't a big deal, but seeing all the other parents and grandparents holding flowers made her feel awkward.

Her granddaughters did not run up and hug her—they didn't even speak to her—but they did hug their Uncle Josh with great relish. "It's hard to watch their relationship with him, and how they don't light up when they see me," Brown says. "Well heck, they don't know me. They don't know this person at all."

The worst part was that Josh barely spoke to his mother either that day.

Before the show was over—but after her granddaughters had completed their part—Brown whispered to Alana that she was leaving. It had been a long workday and she was tired, she said. That was only half the truth.

"Alana couldn't understand how painful it is to sit three seats down from my son and he doesn't even acknowledge that I'm there," she says. "I don't think anyone can comprehend the depth of pain...to have someone so close to you and not even be able to touch him. Or talk. For fear of—I don't even know what.

"In prison, I dreamed of things that I'd do with my kids. It's just not realistic, because they've gone their ways—which is not necessarily a bad thing—but there doesn't seem to be any space in there for me."

Yet Brown counts her blessings, because she's free and she's healthy. Her health is especially miraculous because back in Draper, a year after doctors removed her right breast to get rid of the cancer, they found a whole other batch of cancer in her cervix.

Brown cracks up telling this story, which really isn't funny at all.

After being diagnosed with cervical cancer, her oncologist asked how she was doing on the tamoxifen citrate he'd prescribed a year earlier to keep her breast cancer from returning.

"My what?" Brown asked. She didn't know anything about tamoxifen. Somehow the prescription had never made it to the prison pharmacy.

"The doctor went crazy on the telephone with the prison officials and they actually did end up getting it for me. But at that point I had cervical cancer," Brown says, laughing.

The doctor removed the affected portion of her cervix and she went back to prison and recovered. The sickness never recurred. And her unlikely survival has left her with a giant question: why did God let her go to prison and get cancer, only to cure her and eventually free her?

Is my purpose in life just to survive? she wonders. That seems unlikely. Yet she feels her accomplishments don't measure up to exonerees who have done remarkable things with their lives since getting out of prison. She's particularly in awe of Kirk Bloodsworth, the Maryland man who was the first person to be freed from death row and who went on to become a famous anti-death penalty advocate.

"I'd like to tell you I've accomplished big things since I've gotten out," she says, "but the biggest thing I've accomplished is just nailing a good job and finally getting some stability.

"I've been preserved and I just don't know what for."

Chapter 4

CORNELIUS DUPREE
Texas, 30 Years

After his first crushing rejection from the parole board, a soft-spoken Texas man serving a staggering seventy-five years for a crime he didn't do—robbing a young couple at gunpoint—learned that if you don't lock hope in a box and bury it, it will bury you.

But nearly a quarter century later and up for parole for the fourth time, he felt hope once again burning deep in his gut like wildfire. This time he wouldn't go before the parole board as usual, but before Rissie Owens, the parole commissioner herself. This was no small matter. Every inmate knew that when Owens called you up, you were all but guaranteed a ticket to freedom.

And so, one day in 2004, he stood at attention before Owens in the same Texas Corrections-issue white shirt, white pants, and tennis shoes he'd been wearing every day since he was convicted twenty-four years before.

Owens asked him his name and his six-digit Texas Department of Corrections number. He stated both with equal gravity, "Cornelius Dupree. Thirty, eighty-three, ten."

Then Owens asked him to tell his version of the events that led to his arrest. Dupree, as always, refused to say that he and an acquaintance named Anthony Massingill robbed a Dallas couple at gunpoint, kidnapped the twenty-six-year-old girlfriend, and took turns brutally raping her before sending her on her way. All that would be a lie, and Dupree never lied.

"I can't do that because I don't know anything about the case," he said in his southern drawl. "I was just on the street in 1979 and they arrested me and my friend for carrying a bag of marijuana. They gave us seventy-five years."

"You have no knowledge of what happened?" Owens asked.

"No, ma'am."

Owens contemplated that for a moment. If anyone was feeling the brunt of prison overcrowding in Texas, it was she. Owens told Dupree she was sympathetic; he was just a kid when he was locked up. He lost both his parents. He lost a lot of things.

"Give me a reason I should grant you this," she said.

Dupree gave her more than one. "First of all, ma'am, I didn't commit the crime. I've been here since I was nineteen years old. I missed my parents' lives. I missed my twenties, my thirties, and my forties. I feel like I deserve to go home and become a productive citizen."

Another pause. Owens said she would consider granting Dupree parole. *Would consider*, Dupree thought to himself, *words I've heard before.* But never from the commissioner. In his mind flashed the image of his fiancée Selma Perkins in a wedding dress.

"But on one condition," Owens said.

"What's that?"

"You will be released on the condition that you complete a sex offender program."

Sex offender program? Dupree was startled—somewhat. Yes, he'd been charged with rape back in 1979. But the rape charge was dropped after he was convicted on the armed robbery. So as far as he was concerned, joining a sex offender program would be like enrolling in clown school to get out of prison.

"Excuse me, ma'am," he said, "I'm in prison for robbery—a robbery I didn't commit. Nowhere in the course of this time was it ever mentioned that I'm a sex offender." So why, he asked, should he enroll, effectively admitting he was a rapist?

"It states in the report that a sexual act had taken place," Owens said.

"Yes, I understand that may be in report," Dupree said, "but I wasn't found guilty of that."

"That's the law. Those are the guidelines," said the woman for whom guidelines were all that stood between order and chaos.

Fake it till you make it is a motto commonly heard in lockups. It means if the parole board says, "Get on all fours, bark like a dog, and you're free to go," you don't just get on all fours, but wag your tail for good measure.

But for a wrongly imprisoned man like Dupree, integrity factored into every decision he made. Dupree survived his horrific circumstances because he clung to the knowledge he wasn't one of *them*. The rapists. The killers. He was just an honest kid who was minding his own business when the good Lord threw him a knuckleball.

"I don't like to use the term, *friends*," says Dupree when asked who his buddies were in prison. "I wouldn't try to make friends with any guilty party. I did become up close and personal with some guys I played basketball with. I did get to know people on a personal note. But they weren't people I'd bring home and introduce to my family."

Unlike those guys, Dupree was only pretending to be an inmate. Enrolling in sex offender classes meant doing as the guilty do. And that he could not accept.

Any time he was in a jam, Dupree would always do two things: pray and write a letter to Selma, who served simultaneously as his fiancée and his priest. Selma visited him a few days after his meeting with the commissioner, and they spoke on phones with glass separating them. Selma talked animatedly about how thrilled she was for Dupree to come home.

"I can't do it," he told Selma. "I can't go to into that program and admit something I didn't do just to get out." The more he spoke, the more his voice became fiery like a Baptist preacher's. "I'm someone who believes. I'm a God-fearing person. I believe the truth will set you free!"

She responded, simply, "I know you'll do the right thing."

Dupree had had years to soul search at his leisure, but now, facing the biggest moral crisis of his life, he had no time to think. *What if I just enroll?* His mind was like a slide show of snapshots from a potentially very near future: there he was, hugging and kissing his eight brothers and sisters; stuffing a big forkful of welcome home cake into his mouth; exchanging wedding vows with Selma.

He wavered, and wavered some more. That cake looked so real he could almost smell it. "I wanted to go home. I'd been there for twenty-four years. My fiancée wanted me to go home. I was tired of prison," he says. Dupree reluctantly agreed to fake it till he made it. "I was willing to see how far I could go. If I could go through it without saying, 'I'm a sex offender. I did the crime.' If I could have gotten off that way I would have tried. I wanted to see how much I could endure. Being affiliated with those guys there for that particular sentence…" Dupree trails off, then tries again. "I accepted the fact that I was willing to go to that place."

The sex offender program was like Alcoholics Anonymous, only instead of twelve steps there were the four *r*'s:

recognition, remorse, restitution, and resolution. Dupree gritted his teeth and withstood each day like it was prison within a prison.

Then, about two months in—somewhere midway through the recognition step—Dupree's counselor told him that his moment in the spotlight had arrived: he'd advanced to where he would admit, before a room full of sex offenders, that he'd raped a woman in 1979.

"Hi, my name is Cornelius Dupree, and I'm a sex offender," he'd have to say before walking his audience through every depraved detail, as classmates nodded their heads in solidarity. His counselor advised him if he really wanted to impress the parole board—who'd review his report upon "graduation"—he'd embellish the sick details to make his "crime" seem even worse.

"You had to maximize; you had to name it more than it really was," Dupree says. "Say your case read that you just *touched* someone. You had to say you *fondled* him.

"I explained to my counselor that I was innocent and I don't know anything about the case, so I can't explain anything about it. But the counselors are under the impression that everyone is guilty. So when someone says he's not guilty, it's like, 'We hear this all the time. You are no different.'"

The counselor pulled out Dupree's case file and quickly leafed through it. Then, echoing a line Dupree had heard many times, he said, "You have to do whatever you have to do to go home."

"You're asking me to lie?" Dupree asked.

"You do whatever you have to do to go home."

At this darkest moment, everything suddenly became serene in Dupree's world. His despair let up and he felt calm and clear-headed—like his old self. He made a decision he wished he'd made two months earlier. "I refused to do it and that was it," he says. "I was written up for various disciplinary cases, struck of eligibility for parole, and sent back to prison." It would be another six years before Dupree finally got out.

But it was worth it.

"It was already a war that I was having within the system. That was another phase in it. I was already equipped to stand up to do whatever I had to do to stand my ground. Saying you're a sex offender is much easier to do when you're actually guilty. Because you're really not faking it when you're guilty."

Cornelius Dupree's three-decades-long nightmare began one cool Dallas night in November 1979, when a woman and her boyfriend, both white, stopped at a liquor store to buy cigarettes and use a pay phone. As they were going back to their car, two black men walked up to them, one brandishing a gun. They demanded money, then got into the car with the couple, and ordered the boyfriend to hit the gas.

After a while, the carjackers told the boyfriend to pull over, and when he did they kicked him out of the car. When the woman attempted to flee, they pulled her back inside. The gunmen drove her to a nearby park and then took turns raping her at gunpoint. When they were done, they began arguing about whether or not to kill her as she listened in terror. Finally they agreed to spare her life, but not before snatching her rabbit-fur coat and driver's license. They warned her if she talked to police they would hunt her down. Then they let her go and she ran for her life. She fainted by the side of a road, where a police officer found her.

One week later, a young man named Anthony Massingill invited Dupree, the nineteen-year-old son of a laundromat owner and second-oldest of nine kids, to a party. There would be plenty of girls, Massingill promised. Dupree wasn't particularly good friends with Massingill—their main connection was that their mothers were neighbors—but he was up for a good time.

Dupree was a typical nineteen-year-old. He loved to play basketball and shoot pool, but he'd also reached that age where you catch the faintest glimmer of your mortality and start thinking about doing something with your life. He was looking into joining the Marine Corps.

As he and Massingill were about midway through the twenty-minute walk to the party, a police patrol car pulled up next to them and an officer asked where they were going. "A party," they said. The officer and his partner got out of the car and ordered Dupree and Massingill to stand against a wall, where they frisked them. They found a bag of pot on Massingill.

"When they found that, they continued to shake us down to see if we had anything else," Dupree says. "Lo and behold, my friend had a .22 Derringer." The gun was similar to the one described by the couple who'd been held up a week earlier. Massingill and Dupree were arrested, driven to the police station, and locked up in different cells. They were there for two days.

"At this point I was almost certain I was going to get out because I didn't do anything," Dupree says. Officers brought the rape victim and her boyfriend to the station to look at a photo lineup, and she picked out Massingill and Dupree. Her boyfriend did not pick out either man when showed the same photos. It didn't matter; police booked each man on two counts: aggravated rape and aggravated robbery.

"I have to say, I was somewhat shocked," Dupree says in his typically understated way. "I became numb at being accused of something like that." Still, he kept a level head by thinking about a hero of his who represented all that was just in the world. "Back then, I was a fan of Perry Mason. I really liked the way he won his trials. I really believed in the justice system, that the truth will always set you free. I stuck with that."

As Dupree sat in jail for the next nine months awaiting trial, investigators continued building their case. They found sperm in the victim's vaginal smear slide, which confirmed the woman's account that at least one of the thugs had ejaculated during the rape.

Meanwhile, Dupree hung on to the belief that detectives would find the real bad guys and let the two innocent men free. "I was looking forward to the time of trial, so they could point me out and say I wasn't the guy."

When the trial finally got underway, the issue of both victims' eyesight became a subject that defense attorneys would return to again and again. The boyfriend explained that he'd misidentified Dupree and Massingill in the card lineup because his vision was impaired. And during the girlfriend's cross-examination, she misidentified a photo of both defendants, even though both were sitting right there in the courtroom. She also admitted she hadn't been wearing her glasses for nearsightedness during the attack.

In addition, two women who worked at the store where the rapists tried to sell the victim's fur coat did not identify either defendant in photo lineups. These might have seemed like convincing reasons to acquit. But on April 3, 1980, the jury found both men guilty of aggravated robbery and slapped them with seventy-five years in state prison. The prosecutors dropped the rape charges because a rape conviction would not increase the two men's sentences. They were effectively convicted of rape anyway; why else would they receive virtual life sentences for stealing some money and a rabbit fur coat?

"I felt like this was a dream that wasn't really happening—but it was happening," Dupree says. "I was just stuck. I was just mesmerized. Seventy-five years. Everything inside me just dropped. My face, my heart, everything. That was the most stunned feeling I'd ever encountered."

That terrible day, Dupree learned the first of many important lessons as a convict: Perry Mason is only fiction.

"I felt the reality of how the system actually worked. You're guilty until proven innocent. Once you're in the system, the burden of proof is on you," he says. But something in Dupree sensed that he wouldn't die in prison. "I don't know if it was me being young. I don't know what it was. I just felt like I would make it out. I would see another day."

"When you go in there, you don't know what to do," Dupree says of the hostile new world he found himself—at the maximum security H.H. Coffield Unit, the largest state prison in Texas, where he'd spend his first seven years of incarceration. "But you don't want to be so obvious that you're lost, so you just kind of follow the next person."

Dupree started at the very bottom of the employment ladder, picking cotton for five years. "Backbreaking work," he recalls. "You have to kind of straddle the rows of cotton and pull carefully because the bolls have pointy ends, and if you're not careful you stick yourself." When it wasn't cotton-picking season, Dupree did other outdoor labor— chopping down trees, cutting grass with old fashioned non-electric mowers, and picking cucumbers and watermelons in the garden. "You had to put muscle behind it. It was like when they used to have chain gangs busting rocks. It wasn't as bad as that, but you still had to go out in the heat."

Those first years laboring outdoors were the hardest psychologically for Dupree. He'd always been mellow by nature, but now he felt like a young bull getting constantly taunted by the red capote. "I was very angry, very rebellious towards the system. I was still trying to embrace being here, but I was taking it real hard. A lot of the officers were about my age or sometimes younger, sometimes seventeen years old, and they were telling me what to do."

One sweltering day, Dupree thought an inmate had looked at him the wrong way, so he broke the guy's nose and cheekbone. For that, he was locked in a pitch black cell for two weeks, alone with his thoughts. "In solitary, you don't know if it's day or night. You're weak. You're cold. You sleep on steel. They give you a blanket that's not even a whole blanket. They give you a full meal every third day—cold grits, a cold, boiled egg, a cold cup of coffee, and a cold biscuit. Otherwise you just get a spoonful of rice, a spoonful of grits, whatever it may be."

That would be the first and last time Dupree would ever go in the box. He became the model inmate in each of the seven Dallas-area prisons he did time in, treating every day like a workday in the civilian world: get up, put in a good day's work, come home. He got promoted to cook, then clothing presser, book keeper, and janitor.

He spent most downtime alone. "You go into a dayroom and just sit by yourself," he says. "The thing I learned early on is you stay out of other folks' business."

With so much time to think, Dupree struggled with knowing there was nothing to differentiate him, the innocent one, from the rest of the inmates. Everyone came with the same tagline, "I didn't do it."

"There is no outer difference between the guilty and the innocent," Dupree says. "You all wear the same clothes. If you say, 'Hey man, I didn't do anything,' you get, 'That's what they all say." The only difference between me and them was the struggle within—and that's the part nobody sees."

He found an outlet for his inner struggle in the paperwork he'd file regularly for his case. "I knew there was nothing I could say to the guards or the inmates to substantiate my claim. All that would have to be done on pencil and paper to the court," he says. "When I filed writs and motions and everything like that, you put all your hope on those writs. I filed three petitions for a writ of *habeas corpus*. They were denied, but I was always filing, trying to be heard. I wrote letters to numerous organizations trying to be heard. I requested DNA tests, blood tests, anything. They were denied as well."

After years of denials, Dupree's morale hit rock bottom. "You write all these letters, you're reaching out to people, and you come to find out that people can't help you. You're at your lowest point. You're in the cold, dark cell, alone. No friends no family, no one.

"At that time you have to make a decision. You can continue going down the path you're going or choose another path. And I chose the path of Christ. My faith in God is what kept me strong, kept me secure, got me out of there. I give all praise to God for keeping my health and sanity. If you lose either, you're doomed."

The comfort Dupree found in God went hand-in-hand with his love for a woman who believed in him. A decade into his sentence, a guard he was tight with told him about a woman corrections officer at the John M. Wynne Unit in Huntsville who shared much in common with Dupree— particularly his fervent Christian values. Her name was Selma Perkins. Dupree wrote her a letter introducing himself, and she wrote back. Soon they were exchanging four letters a week and would talk on the phone every other night.

"Don't get me wrong, it was costly, using those tele-phones," he says. "But that was my support system. She was there when I didn't have anything and was at my lowest. I needed a good woman who would love me and appreciate me for me. She had a demeanor about herself, so God-fearing, and that's number one. I knew at some point I was going to be released. I didn't want someone who was still going to clubs and liked to party, drink, and smoke."

For twenty years, Selma faithfully visited Dupree every chance she got, often maxing out the monthly allotment of three contact visits and one non-contact visit. These get-togethers were no romantic picnics at the park, but the couple's mutual faith in God kept the courtship strong. "You have to have faith and hope and pray that this will turn out positive," Dupree says. "She didn't know if I was guilty or innocent, but she got by on her faith to stand her ground and support me."

Dupree served out those six extra years for quitting the sex offender program with a clear conscience. "After they turned down my parole and sent me back to prison, I felt relief," he says. "If a man doesn't have something worth dying for, he doesn't have a reason to live. To stand up and say you did one of the most hideous crimes you can commit. I believe it was a test from God. If you believe in and trust in God, the truth will set you free."

Right around the start of those six years, Dupree had a conversation with some inmates in the library at the maximum security W.J. Estelle Unit in Huntsville that would change the course of everything. "There were some guys who had read if you can prove your case with DNA, that lawyers would take your case pro bono. So, I figured, why not? I really didn't think there was any DNA available because my case happened in '79, but I didn't have any-thing to lose."

He wrote a letter to the Innocence Project in New York City. "I explained to them if you show I didn't commit the rape, you prove I didn't commit the robbery," he says. Overloaded with other cases, it took the Innocence Project two years to write back. They agreed to sign Dupree, and asked him to send over all the paperwork he had.

The lawyers' only hope of winning meant getting a hold of the physical evidence used in Dupree's trial and testing it for DNA. The Dallas County District Attorney's office agreed to conduct a search for the evidence but eventually concluded the victim's vaginal swabs had been lost or destroyed. The office was only able to find clippings of her public hair. This wasn't promising, but it was something. Moving at a snail's pace, the District Attorney's office in 2009 finally permitted the Innocence Project to test the hair samples.

In July 2010, still awaiting the results, Dupree was paroled—a joyful moment dulled by the fact that he wasn't really free.

"I came out as any other inmate on parole. I had the ankle monitor on me, so I couldn't just go to the grocery store or walk to the park. I couldn't even walk in my yard without permission."

Even worse, he had to enroll in yet another sex offender program.

Ten days after he got out, the DNA lab issued a report that, to the lawyers' shock and delight, disclosed that a large amount of sperm cells were found on the pubic hair—cells that did not come from either Dupree or Massingill.

Since the rape and robbery were committed by the same two men, this proved that neither convict was guilty of either crime. It was a momentous revelation—muted by Dupree having to keep reporting to parole as the legal process slogged along. "Once they set a court date, the whole world would know I was an innocent man."

In the meantime, Dupree could at least fulfill another dream that was decades in the making. He and Selma finally got married, amid a small group of relatives at Selma's home. Selma looked radiant in a pink dress. Dupree wore a modest but becoming shirt and slacks, the ankle bulging out because of the electric monitor. The newlyweds exchanged simple gold wedding bands—they were all Dupree could afford—and celebrated over a cake decorated with the words "Selma and Cornelius, Married: July 31, 2010."

On January 3, 2011, Dupree put on a dark suit and went to court to be declared an innocent man. He stood before Judge Don Adams alone, without codefendant Anthony Massingill, who was still in prison on a second rape conviction (Massingill maintains his innocence in that case). At the end of the short hearing, Adams told Dupree, "You're free to go." Outside the courthouse, a beaming Dupree told the TV cameras, "It's a joy to be free again."[1]

"That was a moment I'll never forget," he recalls. "It was a moment that really declared me a free person. You have to have your freedom taken away from you to understand what I mean."

But even after that momentous day, Dupree had to make one more demoralizing hurdle, thanks to the state's crippling slow-footedness in filing the exoneration paperwork with the Department of Parole. A week after they exonerated him, he went back to Houston. There, he got a call from his parole officer, telling him he needed to come in and report.

"Excuse me, ma'am, I've been exonerated," he said.

"Yes, I know, I saw it on the news," she said. "But I don't have any paperwork. So you need to come in and report."

Dupree was speechless. He says, "That meant I was still under house arrest; I still couldn't go anywhere; I still had to have a monitor on me; I still had to go to the sex offender class and pay twenty dollars to sit there for three hours."

His voice rises as if he still can't believe it.

"When a judge sets you free, you feel like you should be free!"

At the time, Dupree was interning for Texas State Senator and Innocence Project Board Chairman Rodney Ellis, and asked the senator to intervene. Ellis did, and Dupree soon found himself testifying before the Chairman of the Criminal Justice System—who was horrified by what he heard.

The chairman ducked into chambers. A few minutes later he reappeared and told Dupree that he would no longer need to report to parole. Surrounded by fellow exonerees who came to show support, Dupree told the chairman, "At this point in time, I feel like a free man." The room burst into applause.

As a last order of business, they removed the ankle bracelet. "I felt the weight of the shackles being taken off me," Dupree says.

Dupree successfully sued the state for $2.4 million—more money than he ever imagined having. A chunk of the winnings went toward a house in Houston and a shiny new DTS Cadillac. He also splurged on new wedding rings for Selma and him—both encrusted with diamonds.

Every morning, Dupree works out at a YMCA gym, and every evening he prays with his church group. He works for Tools for Teens, a Christian organization that visits juvenile jails and gets boys to straighten out while they're still young. "I get a joy out of that," he says. "It gives me an opportunity to go in there and redirect those guys' lives. I call it a crossroads. If I can touch them, get into their hearts and their heads, that can be a very significant turning point in their lives. I try to tell them about my losses in prison. I lost my twenties, thirties, and forties—and my parents."

An agnostic might be skeptical over how little Dupree appears to struggle with having lost all he did. "When God's plan intervenes, that's the way it is. There's nothing we can do about it," he says—words a non-believer might find naive.

Well, it's not naive at all.

In prison, Dupree learned how to unburden himself of bad feelings by accepting—really accepting—that God decided his fate, not he. Then, his seemingly wasted life felt purposeful again, like he'd been assigned a holy mission. And that was a wonderful feeling.

"It came to my mind that I wanted to get out of prison as soon as possible from day one, but while I was there, God had me there for the reason," Dupree says. "It was a test. I prayed to God that he release me when he was ready.

"What I went through made me who I am. The only way you know your inner strength is to be put to a test. I recall while I was in prison hearing about how Nelson Mandela did twenty-seven years. I said, 'Golly, twenty-seven years! That's incredible!'

"Well, now I've got him beat."

Chapter 5

DRAYTON WITT
Arizona, 10 Years

Drayton Witt was feeling pretty good in those seconds before three Aryan Brotherhood thugs jumped him, stabbing him again and again until his body looked like it had been used for machine gun practice.

He was happy because he had ink on his mind.

Tattoos were his thing. His prison-ripped body was almost entirely covered in dragons, goblins, and tigers. And, in several places, the word "Steven"—the name of his dead infant son.

When the Brotherhood came for him, Witt was sitting on the curb at the rec field of the Winslow Apache Unit in eastern Arizona, three years into a twenty-year murder sentence. He was meeting a guy upon whose chest he'd ink a giant cathedral-style cross.

Someone called his name and he looked to his right.

Then something razor sharp slammed into his left ear with the force and heat of a red hot hammer. The point went deep, puncturing his eardrum and sending exploding pain through his head.

Two seconds later, Witt felt two powerful punctures to his neck and the base of his skull. He understood now. He'd been waiting for this moment since the day he was convicted.

The rage kicked in. Witt pulled out his own knife and lunged at the Nazi trio.

"When I got to my feet and started stabbing the shit out of them back, I think they were very surprised," he recalls. "They figured when most people get stabbed, their first reaction is to run."

The lopsided battle lasted longer than it should have, but maybe Witt wanted to live more than the Brotherhood wanted him to die. He jabbed at one while the other two were hacking at his back and flanks, and then he spun around and jabbed some more. "I stabbed one of them probably twenty-five times," he says, "all over his hands, stomach, back, arms, you name it."

But adrenaline can withstand only so much heavy blood loss. "I went from standing on two feet, swinging and stabbing, to on one knee, to on both knees, to curled up in a ball. Your brain tells your body to move but it don't move."

Two of the attackers, both badly cut up, ran off. The third, a fat, bald Nazi, the one who got him that first time in the ear, stuck around to finish the job. Witt was trying to cover what was left of his face as the Nazi stabbed through his hands.

By the time corrections officers ran over and hauled the hulk off Witt, he had seventy-three wounds in his body, including a severed facial nerve that blinded his left eye. His hands looked like they had gone through a meat grinder and would require extensive reconstructive surgery. "I don't know how the hell I survived."

Apparently even Nazis have a soft spot for babies. So when word got out that Witt was locked up for shaking his infant son to death, punishment was in order.

Fuck him like John Holmes was the message the Brotherhood chief had scrawled on a piece of paper and sent to the yard that day. The yard head assigned three hit men to do the job and prove they were worthy of the Brotherhood patch—a tattoo of a shamrock overlaid with a swastika.

"You're green lit as soon as you go into prison for having something like that on you," Witt says of his baby-murder charge. "It's funny—you get some guy who's in prison for raping some sixty-year-old woman and beating her to death. But he can be a gangster and one of the fellas, and he's not looked down upon. It makes no sense."

Witt found out about the John Holmes letter—Holmes being the name of the prolific seventies-era porn star —when he was placed in protective segregation after returning from the hospital. A Brotherhood member who'd been assigned the hit, but turned it down, showed it to him.

That man had turned down the job because he believed Witt was innocent.

"There were quite a few people who were upset that I'd been stabbed," he says. "Anybody who actually knew about my case knew it was bullshit."

Drayton Witt may have been a violent son of a bitch. But he was no baby shaker.

"I was the kind of guy who if you looked at me wrong, I would get out of my car and punch you in the face in the middle of an intersection," Witt says. "I've been that way my whole life."

Witt's anger began, as far as he can remember, when he was twelve and his parents moved the family from Homeland, California—a hole-in-the-wall town surrounded by mountains, where people rode horses on the street and kids rode motorcycles to school—to the big city of Phoenix.

"I was pissed," he says. "I grew up riding my dirt bike to school, riding my dirt bike on the track every day. And then they moved me out here to the city, took all my toys and I was like, 'What the hell?'"

Witt ran away from home and made friends with people who taught him how to manufacture and sell drugs and to steal cars. He spent as much time in juvie as he did on the streets. When he was sixteen and out on parole, a buddy let Witt stay at his place. Then the buddy took in another roommate, a hot-headed, gun-toting eighteen-year-old stunner named Maria Holt.

Witt was smitten. He wanted her, badly.

One time he tried forcing his way into Maria's room and she wouldn't let him. "If you come in here, I'll shoot you," she said. Then she opened the door and pointed a gun at his head.

Man, I think I'm in love, Witt thought.

They became a modern day Bonnie and Clyde, igniting passion as often as fury in each other. "She was just as crazy as me, but the total opposite," Witt says. "I was just wild in every front—no sense of responsibility—and she went to work every day. She paid the bills. She was grown up."

Then, two months after they met, the couple called it quits after a big fight. Not long after, a rebound guy got lucky and Maria got pregnant.

To no one's surprise, the father bolted. Witt decided he'd step in. "The baby wasn't my blood, but he was mine, no question about it. I had the choice when he was conceived to walk away or not. I grew up without a dad, I knew what it was like. I certainly wasn't go let that happen if I could stop it."

When Steven Witt was born in January 2, 2000, he wasn't breathing properly and doctors found fecal matter in his lungs. They revived him, but he'd suffer respiratory problems throughout his far-too-short life.

After five days Steven's condition improved enough that the hospital discharged him. For the next couple of months, Witt and Maria got to enjoy him as they would any baby—except for the frequent doctor's visits. "He was a cherub," Witt says. "He had so much personality, it's unreal. He was very keen, very attentive. He fed himself from a bottle at two months old. He was big, too; he grew so fast that when he was five months old, he could wear a nine-month-old outfit. The boy probably would have been six feet tall by the time he was ten."

But then things rapidly unwound. Doctors diagnosed Steven with pneumonia and prescribed him an antibiotic. Then the seizures started—the first resulting in six days in the hospital—where his eyes would lose focus and he'd projectile vomit. "We were in and out of the hospital, and they kept sending us home, sending us home, sending us home," Witt says. "They couldn't figure out the cause, but they'd be like, 'Here's some medication,' and kick him out."

Witt was only eighteen and Maria was twenty. "We were a couple of young kids with a sick baby. We didn't know no better; we only knew what we were taught: trust hospitals, they know what they're doing."

On the night of June 1, 2000, Holt was at her waitressing job at Bill Johnson's Big Apple restaurant in North Phoenix when Witt phoned to say Steven might be having a seizure; his eyes were not normal and he was fussy. Maria told Witt to come pick her up and they'd take the baby to Paradise Valley Hospital.

On their way there, Steven had another seizure in his car seat. Then he stopped breathing. Maria took the wheel while Witt frantically performed mouth-to-mouth resuscitation and chest compressions. By the time they arrived at the hospital, the infant was in cardiac arrest. It took doctors thirty-two minutes to get his heart beating.

Steven was helicoptered to Phoenix Children's Hospital, where doctors immediately suspected shaken baby syndrome—a condition identified by three things: bleeding in the eyes, and bleeding and swelling in the brain. The lack of external trauma helped reinforce the belief that he'd been shaken.

The doctors called Child Protective Services (CPS) and the police. Within a half hour of getting the call, cops were already at the hospital questioning Witt and Maria.

"They were already treating me as a suspect in a homicide and my son was on life support in another room," Witt says. "I immediately began to be aggressive."

He told the lead detective, "Get the fuck out of my face."

When the sun rose on June 2, its cheerful light put no color in Steven's parents' sallow faces. Later that morning, they both broke down crying when the doctors informed them that the baby was brain dead. Witt and Maria spent a few hours rocking their son and whispering their good-byes.

Finally, the doctors pulled the plug. Steven died in Maria's arms.

At that very moment downtown, Child Protective Services and the County Attorney were preparing a case against Witt.

When the couple dragged their spent bodies out of the hospital that afternoon, they discovered that cops had towed away their car as evidence. Friends gave them a lift home, and when they got there police were already inside, with a warrant in hand, ripping up carpet and emptying drawers onto the floor. "It looked like our house had gone through Tornado Alley," Witt says. Investigators bagged whatever they needed, including photo albums of Steven.

The next day, the medical examiner Dr. A.L. Mosley conducted an autopsy and confirmed there was no trauma external to the infant's body. He found bleeding in the eyes and bleeding and swelling in the brain. He concluded this was a textbook case of baby shaking and ruled Steven's death a homicide.

For the next five months Witt and Holt grieved at home. "We became hermits," Witt says. "We didn't leave the house. I don't think either one of us cared much about life at that point. All I did was watch TV and get high. That's pretty much what Maria did for a while, too."

Meanwhile, investigators quietly built their case. "They were questioning everyone who knew me, trying to make me out to be some crazy psycho monster. They were successful with having people say, 'He's very violent, short tempered, hot headed.' I was.

"But just because I'm aggressive toward other grown males, doesn't make me someone who's going to backhand a child because I don't like the way he's eating a hot dog."

Many women would have left their partners under these circumstances, but Maria stood by her man. "It's funny," Witt says, "because one of the things she's always said was, 'If I thought for a second that he was capable of doing that, they'd never have a chance to arrest him; I'd kill him.' It always made me laugh. You look at her, a five-foot-two, one-hundred-thirty-pound girl. But those aren't idle threats; those are real. She'd put a gun to my head and pull the trigger."

In November 2000, Witt heard a loud knocking on his door. "I know a cop's knock. I knew it was them," he says. The police asked Witt to come with them to the station. He refused, and they handcuffed him.

"When I got there, they were like, 'You know what you did. You're being charged. You're a fucking scumbag.' At that point, I was pretty much like, 'Fuck you. Go fuck yourself.' That was pretty much my answer to everything."

Authorities charged Witt with first-degree murder and child abuse and sent him to a dingy, filthy hellhole called Madison County Jail. He couldn't make the cash bond of $125,000 so he stayed there for fourteen months.

Jail was windowless and overcrowded, with inedible food and nothing to do to distract oneself. "In county jail, you never see the sun, whether you're in your cell or not," Witt says. He'd have gone crazy if not for the sedating—and nauseating—effects of pruno, a nasty jailhouse moonshine made from fermented fruit.

"You'd hear all these guys in county jail who've been to prison who'd be like, 'Man, give me a plea so I can get back to the joint. I hate this place.' And you always wondered why they said that. But when you got to prison you understood—'Oh wow, this is fucking Camp Snoopy!'"

Witt only weighed 120 pounds, but he was a bulldog. If someone looked at him the wrong way, bumped into him and didn't say, "Excuse me," he'd sic 'em. His specialty was breaking noses and jaws.

He also turned his aggression toward what later became a passion: bodybuilding. In his cell he'd do push-ups, squats, and curls. He'd even bench press his cellie who'd be balanced on a broomstick that Witt lifted.

Witt was confident that he'd be acquitted at trial. "I thought there was no way in hell any intelligent person would send me to prison for some shit I did not do," he says. "There's no possible way. People are not that stupid." He turned down a plea deal more than once.

Witt had put on twenty pounds of muscle by the time his trial finally came in February 2002, at Maricopa County

Superior Court. He clenched his jaw shut as Prosecutor Dyanne Greer ripped him apart in her opening statement, at one point comparing him to a gorilla.

Five doctors, including the medical examiner, testified that Steven's symptoms indicated he'd been violently shaken. They had no reason to think otherwise; a seminal paper in the *British Medical Journal* had set the standard for indicators of shaken baby syndrome in 1971. In thirty years, no one had ever questioned it.

Against that all-star lineup of physicians, the defense's only batter was Karen Griest, a forensic pediatric pathologist from New Mexico. Griest said Steven could have died from dehydration. She also said shaken baby syndrome research was evolving, and its criteria were not as clear-cut as was commonly thought.

"The worst part was I didn't understand half of what was being said," Witt says. "If I knew then what I know now, I would have hit the books and learned the stuff. I was so naive to think that, hey, man, these people will get it right."

Witt kept believing they'd get it right until a millisecond before the jury foreman opened his mouth and said, "Guilty."

"If I was a bomb, I would have blown up at that point. That guilty verdict gave birth to a very very nasty person. They validated all those nasty things they said I was. They created a monster."

That night, Maria came to visit Witt in jail. "I was so bitter and so hateful," he says. "I even told Maria to leave, to forget I exist, to just go on with her life." Maria told him she wasn't going anywhere. "We'll fight this all the way to the end," she said.

In the two weeks between conviction and sentencing, Witt paid for an expensive psychological evaluation, believing this would earn him the minimum sentence of thirteen years. But when he stood up for sentencing, the judge gave him twenty.

"I felt like grabbing the judge and popping his head off his shoulders; I seen murder, I was so angry," Witt says. Yet he had something to be thankful for, too. "I was absolutely thrilled that I didn't end up with life. It's funny when you think about it. Hey, I'm sitting here for something I didn't do, but, oh my God, I'm glad I got twenty years and not life."

Three days later, Witt took a two-hour ride to the first of several prisons he'd call home over the next ten years: Rincon Unit at the Arizona State Prison Complex in Tucson. The guys from county jail hadn't lied; prison was one hell of an improvement. "It was lovely compared to where I'd been," Witt says. "I got to smoke cigarettes, smoke weed, watch TV when I wanted, work out, get tattoos."

As soon as he settled in, he started writing to the non-profit Arizona Justice Project in hopes they'd take his case. The response back was to the effect of, "We apologize, but at this time we cannot take your case because we do not have the funding or the resources."

"I got that same letter for years, and I just kept trying and trying," Witt says. In the meantime, he worked on forging a jailhouse identity. What type of guy, Witt figured, did he want to be perceived as? Easy: the Guy You Never Fuck With. "I learned that violence was a very very good role for me; it worked. I was a little guy, but people would go, 'Watch out for that motherfucker. He's nuts.'

"I stabbed guys in the buttocks if they cut me off in chow line, just to prove a point. It sounds funny, but when you get stabbed in the butt cheek it takes so long to heal, and every time you sit down or stand up it hurts. It's kind of like a reminder: you don't cut people in chow line."

Then one day someone really pissed him off—a big, brawny bully who'd slap younger inmates and swipe their commissary, like the big kid who steals a younger kid's milk money. "I hate bullies," Witt says. "So I took my little crew, me and two other guys, and we beat that dude within an inch of his life."

First they let the thug do his whole workout so he'd get nice and tired. He was on his last set of push-ups and Witt waited for him to go down on the push-up blocks. Then he ran up and kicked him in the face as hard as he could, like a soccer kicker.

"I will say this: that dude is probably the toughest adversary I've ever seen in my life. After smashing in his nose and caving in his eyes, he still stood up on two feet and swung punch-for-punch in the middle of the rec field. He was a beast.

"I knocked him out. When he hit the dirt, I stomped on his head till I woke him up and he got back to his feet. I knocked him out again. When he got to his knees that time, I smashed him in the face with my knee. I broke my kneecap, but that woke him up. Then, when he got up the third time, I stomped on his head until the cops sprayed me with pepper spray and tackled me."

The beat down earned Witt fourteen months in solitary confinement, with just an hour outside the cell three times a week. "It was fucking heaven," he says. "I was locked in a cell probably the size of your garage—just me, my TV, and all my books." He read everything from the works of Plato to L. Ron Hubbard's *Battlefield Earth* ("One of the best books ever written," he says.) He'd watch his two favorite shows, *The Big Bang Theory* and *Masterpiece Theater*.

It was shortly after he got out of solitary that the Aryan Brotherhood hoodlums stabbed him until he looked like a cocktail strainer. By some miracle he survived, but the attack changed him. Made him even angrier.

"It turned me into a pretty cold-hearted son of a bitch," he says. "It totally triggered something in my brain. I had no compassion for human life at that point. Say I'm walking to the chow hall and see somebody sitting in my seat. I'm not even gonna talk to him. I'm gonna stomp his head in the concrete and then eat my dinner and walk away. Prior, I'd maybe discuss it before going to such extremes."

As soon as he was strong enough, Witt got into serious bodybuilding under the guidance of a massively-muscled murder convict named Gunner, who taught him how to work out different parts of his body one week at a time. Witt pumped enough iron to bring his weight up to 225 pounds. "For me it was a way to focus," he says. "When you look good, you feel good. When you feel good, you're in a better state of mind. Prison's a horrible place. They do everything they can to mentally break you. Staying one step ahead of that is very important."

The other thing Witt decided to do after he recovered was to ask Maria to marry him. Ever since he'd gotten locked up, Maria had driven out to see him every week—even when he was transferred to far-off Rincon Unit, or even further to Winslow Apache Unit. She would work an all-night shift and wake up at four in the morning to see Witt, and then drive back and go to work. "She's a rock star, that's for sure. She's that kind of person where if she believes in you and she trusts you and she loves you, she'll give you everything."

It was no dream wedding, but in the end they were husband and wife. He wore his orange jumpsuit. Maria had been warned not to wear a blue or brown dress because those are corrections officers' uniform colors. Nor could she wear orange, because that color was for inmates only.

So she got married in a maroon dress with a T-shirt to cover her bare arms. They read their vows before a pastor and exchanged a brief kiss.

"I don't know if you know prison weddings," Witt says. "You have to pay for your own pastor and they pronounce you man and wife, and it's that quick. She leaves and you leave. It's the most basic, boring, horrible place to get married. You're allowed to kiss, but that's as far as you can go. There's no consummation. None of the good stuff."

Witt heard the words *I didn't do it* a thousand times in those ten years; it was just white noise.

"When you scream, 'I didn't do it,' there's a hundred people next to you that are screaming the same thing," Witt says. "How many times can the boy cry wolf? You get so numb to hearing other people."

Except when the crime involved hurting children.

"You'd get these dudes who are like, 'I really didn't do it. It's fucked up. I'm here for the same reason as you.' And I would tell them, 'Hold on. Excuse me. Break it down for me. Tell me what you're in prison for.' And I used to listen and see if they said the wrong things."

The wrong things?

"One thing that I learned from all the books I read, from all the seminar science, if you hurt a child in any way, they're gonna bruise. Children are more fragile than people understand."

So Witt would ask the dude, "Did the kid have bruises?"

"Yeah, but I didn't hurt him."

To which Witt would respond, "You're fucking guilty. If you come near me, I'm gonna hurt you."

As for his own innocence, he says he didn't care whether anyone believed him or not. Yet he admits being labeled a baby killer made for a lonely life. "If I'm a guy who's

in prison for sticking a gun in somebody's face and robbing him, I'm gonna relate to anyone who's in prison for
sticking a gun in another person's face and robbing him.
But for shaking a baby to death? You can't really talk to
anybody about it.

"Which is why me and Armando got along so well."

Armando Castillo was a Phoenix man who went to
prison for reasons uncannily similar to that of Witt—even
down to the name of the deceased. On June 13, 1998,
Castillo was babysitting his girlfriend's baby, Steve. When
the girlfriend came home, she lifted the baby in her arms
and screamed. Steve looked like he was choking. Then
he passed out. The panicked mother called paramedics,
who found his airways clogged with vomit. He died in
the hospital the next day.

The medical examiner found bleeding in Steve's brain
and eyes. A child abuse specialist examined Steve and
told police he'd been shaken to death. Castillo was the
last person to spend time with Steve before the incident,
which automatically made him the suspect. He was convicted within a year.

Witt and Castillo met in 2006. Witt was doing pull-ups
in the rec yard when Castillo asked, "Hey, is that your
name?" referring to the word "STEVEN" tattooed in huge
letters across Witt's back.

"No, it's my son's name," Witt said.

"Oh, mine too," Castillo said.

They became friends after that, working out next to each
other every day. But it took a while before they discovered they had more in common than sons named Steven.
"When he asked me what I was in for, I told him, and he
was like, 'Wow, really? I'm in here for the same shit.' Our
innocence was the bridge to our friendship."

Castillo had a legal team from the Arizona Justice

Project working on his case, and Witt was still writing letters seeking help from the group. One day in 1998 one of their lawyers, Carrie Sperling, came to see him. At the end of their half-hour meeting, Sperling requested Witt's paperwork and promised to bring it back.

"She pretty much told me when she left that they were taking my case," Witt says.

Over the next three years, Witt and Castillo became each other's cheerleaders as they made slow progress on their cases. "One day he would find something out and he would come to me, and when I would find something out I'd go to him," Witt says. "We would kind of go back and forth about the way they were doing things."

A lot had changed in shaken baby syndrome research since Witt had been convicted, namely the new belief that the "big three" symptoms can be caused by things other than baby shaking—like the seizures Steven had been suffering.

The new research was sufficient to spring Castillo from prison on February 2011. By then, Witt was well on his way to freedom. His lawyers got sworn statements from a number of key physicians testifying that they now doubted the validity of Witt's conviction. Among them was Dr. A. Norman Guthkelch, the ninety-seven-year-old British pediatric surgeon who came up with the baby-shaking diagnosis in 1971. He now wrote in a sworn affidavit that a diagnosis of shaken baby syndrome is "inappropriate as an explanation of Steven Witt's cause of death. There is simply not enough evidence to justify such a conclusion."[1]

Dr. Patrick Barnes, chief of pediatric neurology at Stanford University School of Medicine, concluded that Steven died from venous thrombosis—a blood clot in the brain, tied to the host of health problems he suffered from birth.

"The radiology findings are consistent with the child's history and appear to be natural and/or accidental in nature, with no indicators of non-accidental trauma," he wrote.[2]

Other experts also ruled out the syndrome, most notably Dr. A.L. Mosely, the medical examiner who had performed the autopsy on Steven. After reexamining the case, he wrote, "I have determined that I cannot stand by my previous conclusion and trial testimony that Steven Witt's death was a homicide. Steven had a complicated history, including unexplained neurological problems. He had no outward signs of abuse. If I were to testify today, I would state that I believe Steven's death was likely the result of a natural disease process, not SBS."[3]

In January 2012, Arizona Justice Project lawyers Sperling and Christina Rubalcava visited Witt, as they had been doing regularly for some time. But this time they asked him an unusual question.

"Do you have any Christmas plans for this year?"

"Why would I have plans for Christmas?" Witt asked. "I'm in prison."

"Well, you'd better start making them."

Witt processed that information guardedly, not quite willing to take it to heart, but knowing his lawyers were never anything but truthful. "They never blew smoke up my ass," he says. "From the beginning, they never said, 'I'm bringing you home, I promise. I'll give you the world.' They told me, 'We believe in your case, we believe in you, and we will fight to the very end to get you home.'"

It wasn't long after that conversation that another of his lawyers, Randy Papetti, went ahead and said it. "You'd better make Christmas plans, because I'm going to bring you home." Then Witt let himself get excited. When Maria came to visit that weekend, he broke the news to her.

REUVEN FENTON   111

"Yeah, right. We'll see," Maria said.

"No, really, I'm coming home," Witt said. "All my lawyers told me to make plans for Christmas, so I'm gonna make plans for Christmas. I'm coming home."

Sure enough, on May 1 of that year, Judge Robert Gottsfield granted a motion for a new trial. On May 31, Witt went to court to ask for bond. He was shocked by who he saw in the gallery. "When I walked in there, the whole courtroom was packed with family and friends and people from way back in the day. There were three different bail bondsmen willing to put up whatever was needed. My father-in-law was there. He had every title and deed that he owned."

It turned out none of those titles and deeds were necessary. The judge said Witt was welcome to walk out of that courthouse and go home—free of charge.

"That completely floored me," Witt says. "I was like, 'What the fuck did that crazy old dude just say? Did he really say he was gonna release me with no bond?' Randy Papetti looked over and gave me two thumbs up and smiled. And I'm like, what the hell just happened?"

But until he walked out the door, he was still property of the Arizona Corrections Department—and they made sure he knew that, with their molasses-slow modus operandi. Witt was supposed to be released within twelve hours of his court appearance, so everyone estimated he'd be out by the afternoon, or eight at night at the latest.

As Witt paced around his courthouse cell, Maria sat in her car in the parking lot. Eight o'clock came and went. No movement. An hour passed, and then another. At two in the morning, Witt's attorneys came out to tell Maria she'd better go home and get some rest. But she wouldn't leave, not until the sun came up. At seven o'clock she finally started the engine and headed to work.

It had been a long night for Witt, too. By dawn, his mood had soured. He took his mattress off the bedsprings and leaned it on the bars so officers couldn't see him—because *fuck them*—and let his impolite half do the talking. "You motherfuckers were ordered to release me. You'd better let me go or I'm gonna be the biggest problem you've ever seen!" he shouted. His lawyers, meanwhile, were raising their own hell, arguing to corrections department drones that the judge had ordered their client's release, and holding him against his will amounted to kidnapping.

The noise finally reached the receptive ears of a veteran corrections captain who knew how to expedite paperwork when the situation called for it. He told Witt to give him five minutes. And, amazingly, five minutes later, guards unlocked Witt's cell door and escorted him down the hall and out of the courthouse.

They wished him well and closed the door behind them.

Drayton Witt was free.

But he didn't look free. Dressed in a jail-issue paper suit, he stood alone on the sidewalk, studying the street and sky like a spaceman dumped onto an alien planet. He walked up to a woman and asked her, "Um, can I use your cell phone?" For a second she looked like she'd just met Ted Bundy.

"Are you hurt?" she asked. "Why are you dressed like that?"

"I need to call my wife," he said. "Can I use your cell phone?"

She dialed Witt's wife's number. When Maria heard her husband's voice, she got in the car and hightailed it back to court to pick him up.

They embraced for the first time in the open air in ten years.

Maria asked Witt if he wanted to change his clothes and he said, "I don't care. Just take me home."

So Maria dropped him off at a house he'd never seen

before. Then she left for work. For the second time that day Witt faced his newfound freedom alone, without the slightest idea of what to do next. "That was overwhelming," he says. "I came home, after being stabbed, after being locked in a hole, after becoming the person I became in prison. And now, everything I ever wanted has come to fruition. I've been exonerated. And I'm lost. I've been just fine for the past decade behind bars. I've maneuvered well there; I know everything; it's my environment. And boom, I'm shoved out in the world."

Fortunately he didn't have too much time to think, because one of his attorneys, Erin Ronstadt, swung by to take him shopping. They went to Target, where Witt bought razors, a toothbrush, and other starter-kit necessities for a new life.

Witt was starving. Ronstadt asked him where he'd like to eat. "I don't know," he said. "I've been eating potato chips and tuna for the last ten years. You tell me." Ronstadt picked Abuelo's, one of the better Mexican chain restaurants in town. Witt knew what he wanted the moment he saw it on the menu: the Grande—a kingly meal of three different enchiladas, a cheese chile relleno, a tamale, a beef taco, and guacamole. He cleaned his plate.

Witt was never retried. The Maricopa County Attorney's Office finally filed a motion to drop the case, saying its key expert, the medical examiner, could no longer testify that Steven's autopsy showed he was shaken.

On October 29, 2012, Judge Gottsfield dismissed the charges without prejudice—meaning Witt could never go back to jail for Steven's death and prosecutors could not retry him.

"I can start my life over again," he told a reporter the day his case was dismissed.[4]

And he has.

He and Maria are now the proud parents of a beautiful girl, Ellimae Justice—whose middle name is in honor of the Arizona Justice Project. When Witt cradles her in his arms, he does it so tenderly it's hard to believe this is the same guy who in prison once used his foot to cave in a man's face. "She's my princess," he says proudly. "She's the spitting image of her daddy."

It's strange how babies can be the spitting image of more than one person. The resemblance to her big brother Steven is jarring—and at times painful for her parents to behold. But when Ellimae laughs—and she does that a lot—the pain goes away. Witt is a free man now, and he'll do everything to give his little girl a bright future. He's up at dawn every day, hustling double time to get his housepainting business off the ground. He paints all day and comes home at night, exhausted, but happy to see his beautiful daughter.

"I want her to be able to walk into something at eighteen and not have to struggle in life," Witt says.

He's got another incentive to work hard: to rub it in the state of Arizona's face. "The more successful I become, the worse it is on them," he says. "I genuinely believe that the people who keep poking at me can't handle somebody like me being successful. It bothers them."

Witt took it personally when the state dillydallied dropping his case, even when it was abundantly clear they had no case to stand on.

But if ever there was an incident that could have driven Witt to homicide, it was when Child Protective Services took Ellimae away from her parents after she was born.

One of the doctors at the hospital had realized who Ellimae's father was and called CPS. A caseworker came to the hospital room where Witt was standing with friends and family. Witt asked her what she wanted, and the caseworker said she'd come back the next day. Witt smelled trouble.

The next morning Witt returned to the hospital to bring his wife and daughter home. Hospital staffers told him they wouldn't be discharged until later, because they were waiting on word from doctors. Witt used the opportunity to run to a work site a few blocks away to take care of some things.

Meanwhile, doctors told Maria that they were taking Ellimae for an oxygen test. A short while later, Child Protective Services officials told Maria that they'd confiscated her baby out of fear for her safety. Both parents were a risk, they said—Witt, for his violent, baby-shaking tendencies, and Maria, for having a child with a dangerous baby killer.

When Witt got word, he stormed back to the hospital like the Tasmanian devil. But Ellimae was already gone. CPS kept Ellimae for a shocking *four days*, during which time Witt and his lawyers filed every kind of court paper they could think of.

Finally, someone from the agency called and said there'd been a "horrible mistake," and would Ellimae's family please come pick her up.

At CPS headquarters, Witt, accompanied by Larry Hammond, head of the Arizona Justice Project, notified administrators that they intended to sue the agency. They told Witt that his daughter would be down in ten minutes. But after an hour of waiting, Witt had reached his boiling point. He got into a shouting match with a sheriff who tried to shut the office door on him. Then a supervisor came out and told Witt and his lawyer that there had been yet another "mistake" and they could not return Ellimae.

"That's when Larry Hammond lost his mind," Witt says. "He absolutely blew a gasket. I've never seen a seventy-year-old just go nuts like that."

Supervisors called their supervisors and worked up the chain of command, and then informed the family that the agency had to "clarify some things." Witt hid in some rafters by the building's exit, watching for his daughter. "I was curled up, waiting for them to sneak Ellie out, because I was just gonna clock whoever had her and take her."

Fortunately it never reached that point. As Witt waited in ambush, he got a phone call from Maria—who hadn't left the hospital yet—saying CPS returned the child.

The family went home in a cloud of fury and relief. They have since settled a lawsuit against Child Protective Services.

But Witt still feels like a bubbling cauldron that's about to blow sometimes. "I still struggle to this day with my temper," he says. "I've been home almost two years now and I haven't assaulted anybody, which to me is like the Holy Grail of good behavior. But there's times where I get so angry I'd put my head through a door."

Just talking about the state and all it's done to him gets him fuming.

"The state of Arizona continues to poke me. How long do they expect me to keep being poked? You would think, 'Hey, wait a minute, let's leave this fucking dude alone. He's been through enough.' But they want to keep poking the bear.

"If you keep poking a bear, the motherfucker's gonna swat you. That's how I feel. I want to start swatting now. It's like, what more do you want?"

Chapter 6

MUHAMMAD DON RAY ADAMS
Pennsylvania, 19 Years

He'd think about her all the time, the woman whose lies put him in prison.

Donna Benjamin.

That crackhead, that small time crook, that *nobody*, who told cops he'd shot two men to death, and who swore the same at his trial.

Muhammad Don Ray Adams would think about her every day from inside that grimy Pennsylvania lockup. And he'd pray to God with all his might that she would meet a vicious death.

Sure, there were others who had fingered him as a killer—the sisters Barbara and Darlene Rawls and the rest of them. He prayed for all their deaths. But Donna was something special, because she was the one who had made it personal.

At his trial, Adams sat white-knuckled as he heard her swear that she saw the defendant walk up to drug dealers Darryl Patterson and Thomas Winn in an alley to buy cocaine, and then pull out a gun. She dropped to the ground as Adams blasted them. *BLAM! BLAM! BLAM! BLAM! BLAM!*

Then, she said, Adams looked at her sprawled on the

pavement, begging—*begging!*—"Don't shoot. Don't shoot. It's me."

Her story was the knockout punch to his case. It communicated to jurors that Donna and Adams *knew* each other, that there was no way she might have confused him with someone else.

Hearing her spin such lies, Adams could hold it in no longer. "That bitch is lying," Adams said loud enough for the judge to hear. His Honor told Adams's lawyer to control his client.

"That bitch is lying," Adams said again, louder now. "I ain't killed these people!"

The jury did not give him the benefit of the doubt.

Once behind bars, Adams slogged through the grating process of filing appeals and working his way up the circuit courts, all the way to the United States Supreme Court. And every time he got a denial, he could taste Donna's blood.

"I didn't care how she died," Adams says, "I just wanted her to die."

But Adams is no murderer. He probably could have paid someone on the outside to knock Donna off, but didn't. Only God was qualified to carry out the assassination, and God declined.

And after a very long time, Adams's anger settled and his mind cleared to where he could see the inherent flaw in his prayers.

"I had to sit down and just think about it; maybe I'm going about this the wrong way," he says. "So I started asking God to forgive me for asking him to kill her. And that God would soften her heart and get her to come back and tell the truth.

"And that's what happened."

Before he converted to Islam, Adams was just Don Ray, a kid you'd usually find at the basketball courts near his home in the crime-ridden Richard Allen public housing complex in North Philadelphia. His step-pop was a police officer and his mother was a homemaker.

When Adams was twelve, the family packed up and moved into a row house in the safer, mostly white neighborhood of Logan. Many did not take kindly to the new residents. Racist gangs like the White Boys and the KKK preyed on black kids like Adams.

But over time, as more blacks and Puerto Ricans moved in, the whites moved out. Crime skyrocketed. When Adams was a teen, he got to where he was always carrying a .22, because you'd be a fool not to. One time he and his mother went to church and a kid ran up to Adams with a knife. So Adams pulled the gun out of his suit jacket and pointed it at him.

His mother screamed, "Where you get that from? You gang on?"

"No, I ain't gang on," Adams said. "This is how I go to school."

But Adams has mostly fond memories of Logan, especially of those long summer days playing basketball. "We used to get in cars ten deep and come to your neighborhood and play for a case of beer," he says. "A buddy of mine started a team that went from Logan to South Philly. He called the team *Whip Ass* and the logo was an ass with a whip going across it."

By the time he hit his midtwenties, Adams was apprenticing at a barber shop on Stenton Avenue and Washington Lane called Calis & Smith. He'd been selling drugs on the side for extra cash, but he quit that after becoming a father and converting to Islam. Both he and the boy had the same first name—Muhammad.

Three terrible things happened to Adams in 1990.

The first was he lost his mother to a heart attack the day after her birthday.

Right after he buried his mom, the second terrible thing happened. He was walking around his neighborhood when two guys approached him. One pulled out a gun.

"Whoa whoa, you got the wrong guy," Adams said. "Do you know who I am? I'm Muhammad." Then bullets started flying and he ran for his life. One of the rounds caught him in the hip, lodged in his genitals and stayed there until a surgeon pulled it out.

The third and worst thing that happened to Adams that year was being accused of committing double homicide.

The trouble started early one morning, three days before Christmas, when Adams was cutting someone's hair in his house. He took a break and walked onto his porch, and two brothers from across the street spotted him and asked for trims. Adams told them to come on over.

As the brothers crossed the street, five gunshots rattled off from a couple blocks away. No big deal. In 1990, gunshots were just part of the soundtrack of North Philly. Adams asked one of the brothers to go get some beer while he cut the other's hair. When he came back, he told Adams, "Guess what—they're saying you just shot two people in a driveway." The two people in question were drug dealers Darryl Patterson and Thomas Winn.

"That's a neat trick," Adams said. "I'm sitting here cutting your brother's hair waiting for you to come back and I shot somebody?" Later that night, he went over to check out the crime scene and people were giving him funny looks. The buzz was that someone named Don Ray had fired the shots—a name that came from witnesses who described Don Ray as a light-skinned black man about six feet tall with short red hair. Adams was five-foot-four, dark skinned, stocky, and went by "Muhammad." He did not have red hair.

It's strange, looking back on it, how little that discrepancy mattered to just about everyone involved in his case—witnesses, cops, prosecutors, and jurors.

During their investigation, police interviewed a man named Don Ray who fit the description. He told them he was getting down with a woman at the time of the shooting, and they apparently believed him because they let him go.

Then, that summer, Adams got word that police were zeroing in on him. The witnesses who had originally described the killer as tall and light skinned had changed their stories and were now fingering Adams as the perp. The cops' best eyewitness, Donna Benjamin, said she not only witnessed Adams pulling the trigger, but had a harrowing exchange with him soon after.

"Boo!" he purportedly said, then warned her, "You didn't see anything and you aren't gonna say anything."

Adams reached out to his uncle, a cop, and told him his name was floating around in the homicide investigation.

"Well, did you do it?" the uncle asked.

"I didn't kill nobody, man," Adams said.

"Then don't worry about it. If they come and get you, then I'll be there."

On July 15, 1991, police got a warrant for Muhammad Don Ray Adams's arrest. They smashed open the door at his house but he wasn't there. His frightened sister phoned him at his girlfriend's.

"The cops is here," she said. "They say you killed two people."

Adams called his uncle, who soon showed up with his partner and a sturdily-built young officer. The young officer wanted to put handcuffs on Adams, but the uncle told him to stand down.

When they got to the station, a detective asked Adams if he wanted to give a statement. "Yeah, I'll give a statement," Adams said. "I didn't do nothing. I ain't kill these people and I don't know who killed them. I didn't give nobody no gun. I don't know anything about these murders."

He took a lie detector test. The test administrator told him he'd failed. Adams retorted, "Your fucking machine is broke. I told you the truth, man. I had nothing to do with these murders."

Cops booked him and he was tossed into Holmesburg Prison in northeast Philadelphia to await trial, with bail set at $250,000. His family tried to put down 10 percent so he could walk free; an uncle took out a $20,000 loan, and his immediate family put their home up for $2,000, but they weren't able to scrape together the last of the cash.

So Adams stayed in Holmesburg for a year and a half.

"I'd been petrified about going to Holmesburg because you hear some of these stories about guys who got killed, got raped, got robbed of their stuff, guys who had money sent over by their families to pay off another guy to keep him off," he says. "Everybody in Philadelphia knows about Holmesburg.

"But once I got up there, man, it was like I was still on the street. All my buddies was there. They were like, 'Where the hell you been at, man?' These guys had everything waiting for me—big bags of commissary, socks, underwear."

One day, he and some other Muslim inmates gathered in a cell for prayer. Adams started to cry. "Why did you do this to me?" he asked Allah.

A Jamaican man who led the prayer service approached Adams afterward and asked why he was crying. Adams told him his story.

"Do you think it's a coincidence that you are here on this day of this year?" the Jamaican man asked. "You are decreed to be where you are. You are supposed to be here; I'm supposed to be at this door talking to you."

Then he told Adams his own story—that he'd gotten locked up for killing fifteen people. And he'd accepted Heaven's decree.

"I wiped my tears and I realized God was just showing me there's always somebody worse off than you," Adams says. "And that's how I did my whole bit."

In the fall of 1992, Adams went up for his two-week trial. He dressed spiffily in a black suit and patent leather shoes with black satin bows.

Donna Benjamin, the key witness, was not only a crack addict but had a lengthy rap sheet. But she sounded credible enough while recounting the details of how Adams shot Patterson and Winn.

Adams was unable to produce the two brothers whose hair he'd been about to cut when he heard the gunshots. They had outstanding warrants and could not be found. The only person who could testify to his whereabouts at the time was his girlfriend.

On November 6, he waited fearfully in a holding cell for the jury to reach a verdict. Court officers handed him a turkey and cheese sandwich and orange juice, but his stomach was upset and he could not eat or drink.

It got to be time for prayer. He took off his suit jacket, spread it on the floor, and prostrated himself on it. "God," he said, "Relieve me from this verdict that they find me not guilty."

God decreed otherwise. The jury found Adams guilty of first- and second-degree murder. "What the fuck was you all listening to?" he asked the jury.

"I wanted to cry," he says now, "but I was so angry that they found me guilty for something I didn't do, and here you are going to believe these witnesses who changed their statements from the other Don Ray to me. That hurt."

Back at Holmesburg, Adams went straight to the chow hall. The room quieted down some when he walked in. A friend asked Adams how the verdict went.

"You see what happened—I'm still here with you," he said. "I go back Monday to see if they're gonna put me on death row." He carried a tray of food to a table and just stared at it until the chow hall cleared. Guards got behind him and said it was time to exit.

Back on his block, an officer asked if he needed to move Adams to the front cell, where he could be monitored as a suicide risk.

"Man, get the fuck away from me," Adams said. "That's one sin God don't forgive you for, taking your life. This is just round one. We got fifteen more rounds to go, and this is a heavyweight bout I'm in."

On November 10, Judge Carolyn E. Temin spared Adams the death penalty, sentencing him to life in prison instead. He got shipped to State Correctional Institution in Graterford, where he got his inmate number, BY7451. From there, he went to State Correctional Institution in Camp Hill, then back to Graterford for a few months.

Finally he arrived at the prison he'd call home until his exoneration: State Correctional Institution Coal Township.

The violence was not the worst thing about Coal Township, a 2,300-inmate compound, two and a half hours northwest of Philadelphia. The worst thing was the excruciating day-to-day slog in which *nothing ever happened*.

You could either embrace the monotony as Adams did, or reject it like the might-as-well-be-dead sacks who slept for two-thirds of the day and watched TV for the rest.

Every day, from when Adams rose at four in the morning to when he lay his head on his pillow at ten at night, he labored—either at the law library, studying cases and drafting appeals, or working his jobs buffing floors, doing laundry, or wiring electronics. For downtime he took walks, read Islamic books, and played checkers in the rec room.

"That was my day, every day," Adams says. "You might not want a routine, but you have to have a routine because that's all you can do. If you don't stay busy, you might be one of those cats that killed themselves."

His days were centered around the hope that in the afternoon he'd get mail. "People don't know when you're incarcerated, how important getting mail is. I've seen cellies get upset with other cellies because he's receiving mail and he's not. I've seen cellies hide the other's mail because he didn't get mail.

"I used to always tell my family, 'Send me a Hallmark card. It could say, *Fuck you* at the end, just send me a card. Send me some family pictures, pictures of the neighborhood streets, anything.'"

The best pictures inmates got were the ones from wives and girlfriends wearing nothing but bras and panties (anything less than that and corrections officers, who screened the photos beforehand, would seize them as contraband). Those photos would get circulated around, and over time, Adams collected a photo album's worth from other inmates.

You had to be careful who you showed them to.

"I was out in the yard one day and had some pictures on me," Adams says. "Me and a guy were looking at the pictures and a young guy says, 'Can I look at those?' I said, 'Yeah,' so he started looking at them and said, 'Yo, this is my buddy's ma!'"

During the last stretch of Adams's lockup, he sold off his smut collection at a premium. If someone wanted a really hot picture, he had to cough up a carton of cigarettes. Cash did not exist in prison, but instead took the form of commissary items—junk food, cigarettes, soap, cough drops, deodorant, boxes of cereal, and the like.

Common prison practice is running a two-for-one store out of one's cell—I give you a bag of chips now, you bring me two bags later. His Muslim faith forbade him from selling at such high interest, so instead of getting two bags of chips for one, he'd get a bag of chips and a Snickers bar or anything else of lesser value.

Those deals made Adams a popular merchant, so he was able to afford luxuries like sneakers and his monthly cable bill. The downside to being successful in business was you became a target for corrections officers, who'd seize your stock and write you up if you were carrying more than sixty-five dollars' worth of commissary in your cell.

No problem. Adams was tight with the officers and they didn't hassle him. One time, guards did a routine sweep of his cell. His cellie, a young guy, unwisely threw a fit over them pawing his stuff. "Youngin'," Adams said, "leave them alone, let them do what they have to do so they'll leave the cell." But the cellie wouldn't shut up. The guards did quick surveys of both inmates' stores and saw both stocked more than sixty-five dollars' worth. They hauled off the younger inmate's store and left Adams's alone.

Whether or not you were wrongfully convicted, everyone at Coal Township had a halo above his head. That burned Adams up, because it discredited the truly innocent ones who were working so hard to win back their freedom.

Especially since the liars weren't very good liars.

"You look at their character; their character tells you if they did it or not," Adams says. "It's a gut feeling that you get. Let's say a guy's in for rape. He says he didn't rape nobody, but when he talks about women, he'll say, 'Yeah, I had this one bitch and I did such and such.'

"And I'll look at him and think I believe you *did* rape somebody."

What really ticked Adams off was when a relative or friend of one of the drug dealers he was convicted of shooting would get up in his face and call him a killer. "It didn't happen often, just with different people who just got to prison. They wanted to know about the bodies, and I would give them a look and say, 'Stay out of my motherfuckin' business.'"

Adams got in two fights while in lockup, and both times he threw the first punch. The first happened when he was doing laundry on his block. Someone with connections to Patterson or Winn—Adams doesn't remember which, and doesn't care—asked Adams in a not-very-dignified way why he killed his people.

"I didn't kill your people," Adams growled.

"And next thing I know, I punched him in the mouth and jumped on him," he says. "I just kept punching him till he fell, and I started stomping him."

The second fight happened a year later. Adams was playing basketball with some inmates, one of whom, a tall guy, kept shoving and elbowing him. "Yo, man, whatchu doing?" Adams asked.

After the game, the tall inmate muttered something to Adams about "the bodies," and Adams became livid. "Fuck this," he said and whipped out a shank made of two sharpened pencils taped together. He plunged the weapon into the man's shoulder, pulled it out and sunk it back in again. "I tried to stab this guy till my arm fell off," he says.

"I was really trying to stab him in his neck so I could break the pencils off in his neck."

He did sixty-five days in the hole for that, during which he felt at peace, using the time to study his Islamic books. "After that, I had no more problems," Adams says.

Adams went to prison a healthy man, and came out with diabetes, high blood pressure, cholesterol, sleep apnea, panic attacks, and rheumatoid arthritis. Today he takes fourteen pills a day to treat these ailments.

Some of his problems are genetic—both parents died young of heart problems—but prison without question took away two years for every one year he served. Potatoes, rice, or noodles were the starchy staples at every meal, packing the pounds on his body. Sometimes he tried to eat healthy, skipping chow and eating tuna or salmon he'd bought from the commissary. Or he'd sneak an empty potato chip bag into the chow hall and fill it with salad and bring it back to his cell.

But willpower to eat healthy is hard to scrounge when you're busy fighting off misery—of which he had plenty. And any inmate knows your first line of defense is candy bars, potato chips, and Little Debbie cakes.

High blood pressure came first, followed by diabetes and high cholesterol. Then he started suffering panic attacks, waking up in the middle of the night unable to breathe. "I used to scare my cellie," he says. "I'd wake up petrified and couldn't breathe and he'd be banging on the door like, 'Yo, come get Muhammad, something ain't right!'"

The strange thing was, Adams wasn't having nightmares; all his dreams were about being free.

Adams's son Muhammad visited about six times a year,

and those visits were shots of adrenaline to his father's bloodstream. But they only filled a third of the void in Adams's heart.

Adams had two other kids—a daughter Khadijah and son Brandon—and neither visited him because neither knew who he was. The circumstances of why that was is his own business. But a father is a father, and when you're in prison for life with nothing to do but mull over missed chances, the sadness can smother you.

On Khadijah's sixteenth birthday, Adams mailed her a gift, a cardboard jewelry box that had been covered with faux alligator skin removed from photo album covers. The box's legs and drawer knobs were made from the plastic balls of roll-on deodorant sticks. A photo of Adams wearing civilian clothes was glued under the lid.

He called Khadijah on her birthday and they spoke for the first time. He asked her how school was going. The conversation was a little awkward, but not too bad. They kept in touch after that.

Five years later, Brandon turned sixteen and Adams tried reaching out to him. That was more difficult to arrange because Adams had to first sue for correspondence rights and take a blood test proving he was the boy's father. Once that was done, Adams mailed Brandon's mother a letter saying he'd like to talk to his son at six o'clock on a designated Sunday night. When the night arrived, the mother said Brandon wasn't home.

"I told you I was gonna call," Adams said. "I really need to talk to him."

While they were speaking, Brandon came home. The mother put him on the phone and Adams tried making conversation but only got short answers. *Yes. No. Yes. Maybe.* Adams said he'd like to see Brandon, and he'd like for him to write.

"I need some time," Brandon said. The boy never contacted his father after that. Adams didn't push it.

Donna Benjamin put me here.

"I was thinking of her every day, all day," Adams says—while buffing floors, eating sickening chow, taking showers, pacing back and forth in the hole. Because everything he hated about prison reminded him of Donna.

She, of all people—a purposeless human being who lived to shoplift so she could buy crack. "I prayed and I prayed for God to kill her. It didn't matter how he killed her, just *kill* her."

God let Adams stew for a long time until his anger waned and his heart softened. And when that happened, Adams wondered if God could soften Donna's heart, too. "I started asking God to forgive those that lied about me, and forgive me for my sins too—for asking for their deaths."

The year Adams's heart softened, 2005, was the same year he got his final appeal rejected from the US Supreme Court. There was nothing left to do but resign himself to being a prisoner until his dying day. "If you killed somebody, your ass is supposed to be in jail," Adams says. "Rape somebody, you're supposed to be in jail. I did none of those things, but here I was—in jail.

"If I have to be there for the rest of my life, I want to be by myself."

So he applied for a single cell. The only way to get one was to appear as a danger to others. This was his plan: "I'm gonna wait for my cellie to go to sleep, and—these are the thoughts that are going through my head at the time—I'm gonna bust him across the head with a radio or something. That I'm gonna use the sheets to tie him to the bed."

One day Adams told his son Muhammad on the phone, "Don't come to see me no more, 'cause I'm gonna do something that's gonna put me in the hole for a long time. I don't want you to see me behind the glass."

"No, Dad, don't do that. Don't do that," Muhammad said.

Then Adams heard on the phone a kid in the background, saying, "I wanna talk to my Pop-Pop." It was his oldest grandson, Sharif Muhammad—the same boy who once made his Pop-Pop cry by telling him, sweet as peach cobbler, "I'm gonna be a pro football player one day and I'm gonna come get you out of prison."

Now, Sharif got on the phone and made Adams cry again. "Keep your head up!" the boy barked, like a platoon leader to his men after a rough day in the foxholes. It jolted Adams. "I'm listening to this little kid tell me to keep my head up and it gave me inspiration to go back and keep fighting. The next day, I was back at the law library. I just kept going to the law library, finding anything I could do."

In 2007, encouraging word reached Adams that Donna Benjamin was telling people in the neighborhood that she'd cleaned up her life and wanted to take back what she said about seeing Adams shoot Darryl Patterson and Thomas Winn. But talk is only talk. Adams sent his friends out looking for Donna to nudge her to come clean, but by then she'd disappeared.

Then she resurfaced one day at a block party and told Adams's friend Watts that she was ready to recant—and she meant it. Watts relayed this to Adams.

"Yeah," Adams said, "she said that a hundred times. If she's for real, give her this lawyer's number."

Watts did. And Donna called Adams's lawyer, Terry Pugh, and told Pugh she wanted to change her life, and that meant telling the truth.

Adams had not killed those men, she said. The police had pressured her to testify, threatening to throw her in jail if she refused. She had five warrants at the time for a slew of offenses, mostly shoplifting. So she'd complied out of fear and exhaustion, and because she was on drugs. Now she was getting herself cleaned up, and part of that was making things right.

Pugh persuaded Donna to make her recantation official by writing it down on a piece of paper. And Donna, who never had a speck of credibility to her name, defied everyone's expectations by doing just that. She swore no one offered her money or gifts to change her tune. Nor did anyone threaten her.

God had answered Adams's prayers; following the submission of Donna's letter, Adams got a hearing. But he didn't permit himself joy yet. "You can't get your hopes up so high," he says. "I mean, you're happy and you're blessed that this is going on, that God is giving you this blessing, but you won't feel released until you're home."

His lawyers were not relying on Donna's recantation alone to get him out of prison. They were scouring Philadelphia neighborhoods looking for any and every witness they could find who had anything whatsoever to do with the case.

Adams kept his feelings at bay until his retrial four years later, on April 15, 2011. "For nineteen years and change, I kept on telling people, 'I'm innocent, I'm innocent,' and nobody would ever listen. And when I got in the courtroom and Donna Benjamin got on the stand—she looked at me and started crying. And she looked at the jury and told the jury, 'I lied about this man. He didn't do it.' The feeling I got was thank God they're finally hearing the truth. It didn't matter if they found me guilty or not; she came back and told the truth. I felt so good I started crying."

On April 24, the jury deliberated for two hours. They came back with a not guilty verdict on all charges.

After nineteen years, two more days felt like an eternity when freedom was *this close*. But that's how long Adams had to wait as his release papers made their way from court to the prison in Coal Township, and then to the one in Graterford, where he'd been relocated for his trial. "I made a little noise complaining, but I didn't want to make too much noise because they would throw me back in the hole. If I got to the hole, I wouldn't have access to a phone."

On April 26, Adams was called up to the officer's station. And just like that, a guard told him, "You've got to sign out right now."

This is happening, he thought.

Adams went to the intake unit. As he waited, he gave the officer there a quick summary of the last twenty years of his life, leading up to this moment.

"Man," the officer said, "I've been working here seventeen years and this is the second time I've seen someone get exonerated."

Then he asked Adams, "Can I hug you?"

A guard asking to hug an inmate was about as weird as it could get. Pretty soon other guards came over and wanted to hear his story too. So he retold it, and as he talked he put on the state-issue clothes of a free man—blue khakis, sky blue shirt, navy jacket, and a pair of boots.

Adams signed some release papers. He was taken back to his block to get his property. He made sure to pack his state-issue long johns, which were thicker and warmer than anything you could buy on the outside.

Then officers escorted him outside the prison to wait for his family to pick him up. A lieutenant handed him the cash he'd accumulated on his account. At first, Adams did not know what he was looking at. It had been a long time since he'd seen currency and the designs on the bills had changed. The lieutenant showed Adams how to tell if money is counterfeit by holding it up to the light and seeing if a face shows through.

This was already too much. "Man, I need a cigarette," Adams said. The lieutenant handed him a couple cigarettes and he smoked them on the patio, trying to keep his tension at bay.

Then his family rolled up and Adams smiled widely. They embraced and took pictures using a futuristic looking contraption called a digital camera. During the drive back to Philly, Adams says, "They're all on their phones and everybody wants to talk to me. Now mind you, the only time I've ever been on the street is when I'm going back and forth to court. Now that I'm free, everything is moving so fast.

"I'm on the phone talking to this person, talking to that person. And finally I'm talking to my cousin in South Carolina, and I tell him, 'Listen, man, I'll call you once we get into the house, because everything is moving fast and she's driving fast.' I made everybody shut the phones off, put their seatbelts on and just sit back and be quiet."

The next day a cornucopia of family, friends, and lawyers came out and threw a block party for Adams, complete with a barbecue of the first real food Adams had eaten in two decades—fried chicken, steak, potato salad, mac and cheese. But he barely touched any of it. All he wanted to do was hug people. He had the DJ play "Family Reunion" by the O'Jays again and again.

"I was so happy, really coming to terms with myself that I'm actually free," he says. "I don't have to wait for somebody to tell me, 'All right, chow time! Shower time!

Go in your cell!'" Yet old habits remained. For a long time after getting out, he'd excuse himself from the table by saying, "OK, I'm gonna go take me a shower and go back to my cell."

His relationship with his daughter Khadijah blossomed, but the one with Brandon did not—and may never. After Adams was exonerated, he reached out to his son for the second time. Brandon was twenty-two then. "It was the same thing," Adams says. "He said I was rushing him, so I backed off. If it was me, I would want to see my dad and be with my dad. But that's just me."

Adams was amazed by how much the neighborhood had changed.

"The buses and the trains, they talk to you now," he says. "They didn't do that when I left. I get on the bus to go to doctor's appointments and the bus is telling you every stop that's coming up, and, 'Thank you for choosing us.' I'm like, wow this is all right."

When he went away in 1991, baggy clothing was in fashion. When he got out, it was the era of skinny jeans. "That kind of took me out," he says. "Everybody had on tight jeans. I was like, whoa, what's wrong with these people?"

The nature of crime in Philly had also changed. The bad guys now seemed badder, less respectful of the game. "When I was coming up, you didn't sell drugs around no kids; you didn't sell around old people. When older people were coming by and you're standing at a corner, you'd move out of their way. But nowadays, these young cats don't care what they do or how they sell their stuff. They don't respect nobody."

The brazenness of the bad kids hits particularly close to home. A year before Adams got out, his forty-seven-year-old brother John was gunned down on the sidewalk outside his nightclub, Johnny's Top Cat Club. John was Adams's strongest supporter and his best friend.

One of the gunmen was acquitted; the other was convicted of third-degree murder and sentenced to twenty-five to fifty years. Talking about it now, Adams shakes his head and his eyes darken.

"Both of them should have gotten life," is all he says.

Adams cuts hair only sporadically now because of his arthritis. He's had two knee replacements since he came home. On the bright side, he won a settlement with the city of Philadelphia, and used some of the payout to buy himself a shiny red Cadillac. The license plate says NTGUIL-T.

"There's not enough money that anybody can offer me for doing so much time for something I didn't do," he says.

A chunk of his settlement money goes to prison pals who have no other benefactor. "One of my cellies asked me for some religious books, so I went and got him some religious books. Then he wrote me back letting me know that he received the books, but now he needed me to send him some money because his mom is getting old and she can't do it anymore. I haven't gotten around to him yet; I have to get around to him."

The way Adams looks at it, prison saved his life. Because before he got arrested he had a cocaine habit, a bad one. The kind where you feel like you're possessed and it's someone else's hands cutting the white powder into lines.

"I just didn't know how to stop," he says. "I remember getting high one day by myself, and fell down in prostration. I asked the Lord, "Please, please get me off this." And two days later, I was turning myself in for two murders I didn't do."

Adams hasn't inhaled one speck of cocaine since then. "I don't look at it like I was arrested," he says, "but like I was rescued. I asked God to get me off cocaine, and twenty-some years later I'm off."

So in hindsight, if it hadn't been for Donna Benjamin and her lies, Adams might never have gotten off cocaine. Which is why he's been able to forgive her, and even humor her when she calls him—which she does every month or two, to say she's so very sorry.

"She talks about how it keeps on bothering her," Adams says. "She cries a lot. She cries every time she calls me. She tells me about the things that are happening to her in her life, bad things—her house caught on fire, her daughter got stabbed. Every calamity that happens to her she thinks is the punishment that God is giving her for what she done to me.

"But I tell her, 'Listen, I forgive you. I forgive you and I forgave you. And I asked God to do the same. You have to get on your knees and ask God for forgiveness to relieve you of the demons within you.'"

One of the things Adams used to pray for in prison was to see his little miracle-of-a-grandson Sharif play football. His prayers were answered.

One day, soon after his release, Adams was sitting in the bleachers sipping hot cocoa, munching pizza, and watching Sharif—who's lately been checked out by college scouts—play the game like a pro. Muhammad, the boy's father, asked Adams how he was enjoying the game. The free man could not answer because he was crying.

"What's wrong?" Muhammad asked.

"Do you know how many times I wished and prayed I was here to watch him play football?" Adams asked, weeping. "Just to see him play football."

Adams prayed for so many things in prison that he kept up the habit even when he got out.

"I ask God for so much that I laugh at myself sometimes," he says, "because it'll be like, 'Oh Lord, I know you're tired of hearing from me, but here I go again.'"

Chapter 7

THOMAS KENNEDY
Washington, 9 Years

One December day in 2012, a Washington State man named Thomas Kennedy and his daughter, Cassandra, sat together on a cream-colored couch in front of a live studio audience in New York City to film a segment for Katie Couric's now-cancelled afternoon talk show, *Katie*.

Kennedy was dapper in a blue dress shirt and grey slacks, with his hair pulled tightly back in a ponytail. Cassandra, then twenty-three, looked like teenager wearing grown-up clothes—a buttoned-up brown blazer and red blouse. Couric, elegant in a sleek sleeveless dress and heels, sat in a chair next to them. She asked Cassandra what she was feeling.

"Just embarrassed," Cassandra said, "and just regretful."[1]

What Cassandra was referring to was at age eleven she sent her father to prison for raping her. Nine years later she confessed to making the whole thing up.

"I was just angry and upset 'cause I felt like he wasn't around enough and he…broken promises and stuff like that," Cassandra said. "I wanted more of my dad and I wasn't getting it."

Cassandra cried on and off during the interview, and she cried most of all when talking about Jesus. "There's probably a lot of women out there that want to do the right thing but don't know how, and the way is Jesus," she said. "I wanted to do…I wanted to make it right a long time ago, but I couldn't do it within myself. I didn't know how."

Couric asked Kennedy if he thought Cassandra should be punished.

"I don't think she should," he said. "That's a loving dad speaking about his daughter, of course. Had I been a stranger, probably. Then the bitter, the anger, the resentment, the lifestyle that I lived, I would probably say yes."

Near the end of the twenty-minute segment, Couric asked Cassandra what she'd like to say to her father.

"Thank you for being a good dad and I'm sorry for my wrong perspective as a child about you," she said.

"Thank you for your apology," Kennedy said. "Thank you very much."

The show had gone smoothly, which was a big relief to Kennedy because he'd sensed trouble brewing backstage prior to filming. Cassandra had stood away from her father, arms crossed, with her right foot forward and her weight on her left—the same stance her mother used to take when she'd go to her bad place, with a look in her eye aimed at Kennedy that said, *I. Don't. Like. You.*

Right after the taping, a staffer from the show put Kennedy in a cab along with his two daughters (the elder, Marlena, had appeared in the final third of the segment) and his girlfriend, and sent them to John F. Kennedy International Airport. During the ride, Cassandra was brooding and muttering to herself.

Uh-oh, Kennedy thought.

They arrived at the boarding gate a half hour early and sat down.

And Cassandra boiled over like a pot of split-pea soup on a high flame.

"You son of a bitch," she told her father. "You never should have gotten out of prison."

Kennedy can't remember much of what she said after that. He remembers her words being loud and vicious. He remembers other travelers turning their heads to watch the spectacle.

And this: "You're talking about me putting you in prison for nine years? Well, I'll do it again!"

Wait it out, he told himself. *It's the anxiety. It's not her.*

Sure enough, Cassandra wore herself out after a while, and by the time they were seated the storm had passed. They were laughing and joking when the plane landed in Seattle.

But Kennedy knew what happened in the airport could never happen again.

When Kennedy was seventeen, he met a cute waitress named Susie at the Cozy Nook restaurant in Longview, Washington. She was blond haired, blue eyed, tall and curvy, and four years older than him. She swept him off his feet. He returned every day after school to drink coffee and steal a few words with her.

One night his parents took the family to Cozy Nook for dinner and his dad noticed Kennedy ogling the blond beauty. "You know what, son? You should ask her out," he said. So Kennedy did. Things moved swiftly after that.

"I wasn't thinking in long term," he says. "It might sound kind of redneck, but that's because I'm a redneck—we got married kind of quick."

Marlena was born first, then Cassandra. Kennedy got a job as a foreman for a logging crew, which paid good money. But the hours were long and Susie got resentful.

She threatened to leave with the girls if Kennedy wasn't home more often. The ultimatum pissed Kennedy off mightily, so he turned it back on her.

"If you're gonna take the kids and go, then get out of here," he said.

So Susie left. They got divorced after four years of marriage.

Kennedy would see his daughters every other weekend and during summers when they'd stay with him at his house in Longview. Sometimes, when he picked them up at his ex's place in Kalama, they'd be excited. "We're going to the zoo!" they'd squeal.

But Kennedy had never made plans to take them to the zoo. Susie had hyped them up for nothing, and now their father was the bad guy. What made it worse was that Kennedy knew full well he wasn't much of a dad to begin with, given his habit of getting drunk or high after work. Never when his daughters were around. But still.

Cassandra was the tomboy of the two girls and had a special place in Kennedy's heart. They'd go camping and fishing together, and she wasn't grossed out when slicing open a steelhead and scooping out its guts. She'd sometimes ride the forklift with him at the scrapyard where he worked, and he'd let her push the buttons to operate the shearing machine that cut sheets of metal in half, like scissors to paper.

Sometimes Cassandra would act sullen, so Kennedy would ask her what was wrong.

"I want you to live at home again," she'd say.

Kennedy would answer as gently as he could—but without flip-flopping—"I'm not gonna do it. Daddy's not coming home. Daddy's got his own home and you can come and visit."

One time Kennedy was horsing around with Marlena who was laughing and teasing her father about being an old man. Cassandra, then eleven, was watching the horse-play. She told her sister, "Hey, you need to be nice to Daddy because he's going away for a long time."

Kennedy did not think much about those words. But about two months later, they were splayed across a billboard in his mind when he got a phone call at work from a Longview police detective. Cassandra had told the cops that her father had raped her on three separate occasions at his home.

After Kennedy took a moment to shake off the dust from that bombshell of a revelation, he sputtered, "Well, I'm gonna tell you right now, that's a bunch of bullshit." This was Susie's doing, he said. Susie was afraid Kennedy was going to take the children away from her, and had told Cassandra to lie about her father.

"It hurt my heart," Kennedy says today about what Cassandra had done. "It hurt my feelings, because that's my girl. I would never do that. I would never put her in a situation where she might be around a person who might do that. To be accused of that by one of my kids—it hurt me really bad."

Kennedy went down to police headquarters and sat through a two-hour interrogation. The detective asked if Kennedy would take a lie detector test, and Kennedy said sure. They scheduled one for a few days later.

Kennedy told his father about the test. "You know, son, Cowlitz County's very crooked," his father said. "I suggest we get you a lawyer. You don't want to take a lie detector test without a lawyer present because they're going to screw you." Kennedy hired a lawyer, who immediately quashed the lie detector test. Kennedy wished the lawyer hadn't done that because he would have aced it.

Kennedy heard nothing from law enforcement for the next two months. Then one day the detective called and asked him to turn himself in. Kennedy obliged, figuring the safest bet was to just go through the motions.

On April 19, 2001, the Cowlitz County prosecutor charged Kennedy with three counts of rape. The forecast wasn't good. The criminal complaint detailed explicit accounts from Cassandra about what her father had done to her. She'd even used stuffed animals to play out the attacks. Worse, an examination at a medical clinic revealed that she had trauma to her genitals.

Kennedy hadn't imagined things could escalate like this. How would a jury ever take his word over Cassandra's?

I'm going to prison.

His parents scraped together $10,000 to get him out on $100,000 bond. And Kennedy endured a murky, nightmarish fifteen months awaiting trial. "What was going on in my life was total chaos and destruction. I was just falling apart," he says. He quit his job because of the stress. He lost his house and slept in his pickup truck. And each night as he tried drifting off he'd stare at the truck's ceiling and wonder how his life had gone to shit the way it had.

Kennedy's lawyers told him their legal strategy would be to focus on denial and not on discrediting Cassandra.

"I don't want *denial*. I want *liar*," Kennedy said. "It's not that I'm not denying this. I *am*. But it's that's she's *lying*. It's about her lie. It's not about me doing it."

The lawyer replied, "You don't want to make that little girl look like a liar to the jury."

"Well, why not? She's fucking lying!" Kennedy said.

"Well, if you go try to attack her like that, then they're going to come back on you and think that you're just a bad, vicious man anyway."

The state offered Kennedy a plea deal: thirty-six months in prison and one year probation. He turned it down. Then the state bumped the charges to child rape in the first degree, and came to Kennedy with an even better deal: a year and a day behind bars, with no probation.

"I'm not taking this deal," Kennedy told his lawyer. "You can tell them to kiss my ass."

Then the state bumped the charges up a second time, now to three counts of child rape in the first degree. There was no plea offer this time. It didn't matter; Kennedy could never admit to something he hadn't done.

"That's all I can say—I didn't do it," he says. "I would never give any acceptance to it. I didn't do it. I would never do it. It's not gonna happen, and I'm not gonna give it to somebody."

Fifteen months of waiting for the trial to start, and the whole proceeding took only two days—one to select the jury and one for testimony. The courtroom at the Cowlitz County courthouse was packed.

The prosecutor called up detectives, doctors, Cassandra's teacher—whom the girl had first reported the incident to—and Cassandra's mother. None of those witnesses mattered much to Kennedy, as he anticipated the one who'd testify last.

When Cassandra appeared in the courtroom, Kennedy's first thought was, *I would never let my girl wear that.* She had on a skin-tight yellow dress shirt and slacks.

She testified for about an hour as her father watched from a table ten feet away.

I cannot believe this is happening. I cannot believe this is happening. The words kept repeating themselves in Kennedy's mind.

"It was the hardest hour of my life," he says. "Her demeanor was ice. Revenge. She wouldn't look me in the eye. Even when she pointed at me, she wouldn't look me in the eye."

It was like getting his hand smashed over and over with a hammer and not being allowed to scream. In his imagination he got up from his seat and bellowed, "STOP LYING!" until his throat was hoarse. That hour of silent agony was the worst moment in the entire ordeal, including prison time. "That was my daughter up there lying about me and betraying me. I can cope with doing the time. I can handle that. But listening to her saying what she was saying...I couldn't cope with it."

Those who testified for the defense were mere character witnesses, but they did their best. His parents, girlfriend, and best friend said he was a family man and a good father, and just incapable of doing something so heinous. They spoke the truth. But it didn't matter.

The jury went into a room to deliberate, and filed back out not long after. Kennedy prayed for a miracle.

"Guilty," the foreman said. Kennedy didn't move.

The defense lawyer patted the newly-branded convict on the shoulder and told him, "Good job."

"Don't ever touch me," Kennedy said.

Kennedy was cuffed and taken to Cowlitz County Jail, where he changed into a pair of green khaki scrubs and cocooned himself in his anger. Other inmates knew him as a guy to avoid if they didn't want to get their asses kicked.

Four months after getting locked up, Kennedy was sentenced to fifteen years and nine months in prison. That's what he'd expected and he took the news quietly. But he didn't go to prison right away. Instead, he hired an appeals attorney who got him out on bond while awaiting the appeal results.

During the ten-month wait, Kennedy lived a horrible faux civilian's life. He registered as a sex offender and went to court week after week to attend hearings on his appeal.

He took a job as a dish washer, then as a cook, then as a construction worker. "I couldn't keep it together," he says. "I couldn't maintain a job. I couldn't make cognitive decisions. I just wasn't there. I wasn't functionable. I'd get a job for a little while and I would just explode on somebody and lose it. I would get another job, work it for a week or two or maybe a month and explode on somebody. I'd look back at myself and I'd be like, 'That ain't you. What the hell are you doing?'"

Then he laughs, as he does from time to time when nothing funny was said. "All that anger coming from the hurt within me took a long time to get under control."

Kennedy lived with his mother in Longview during this time, and had been obligated to hang a sign in the window identifying him as a sex offender. One day, hooligans egged the house and broke some windows on his mother's car. He hung a piece of paper next to the sex offender notice that said, If you have any balls at all, come knock on my door and talk to me face to face.

No one did.

One night in August, Kennedy was sitting on the curb on a main drag in town watching a hot rod cruise, where dozens of shiny vintage race cars paraded by with engines revving. Suddenly someone tackled him in a bear hug. It was his daughter Marlena. She said she knew her father was innocent and she loved him.

Sensing it was time to go, Kennedy started walking back to his truck. But it was too late. Cassandra caught his eye from fifteen feet away. She was looking at him. With his index fingers, he made a heart-shape in the air. She did the same.

"I still loved her," he says. "I still do to this day."

Then he saw his ex coming from around a corner, so he got in his truck and took off.

That was the last time he saw his kids for nearly a decade.

The ten-month purgatory ended when Kennedy's appeals lawyer called to say the state had gotten his appeal bond revoked. "Thomas," he said, "they've found a loophole and I don't have a good strong argument to back it up. I'm telling you what: you're probably going to prison."

A few days later he received a reprimand in the mail to turn himself in, and did so on September 9, 2003. He went down to the Cowlitz County courthouse wearing Levi 501s, work boots, and a Bob Seger T-shirt. He changed into scrubs and stayed in a cell for two days before a corrections bus took him to the receiving unit of Washington Corrections Center in Shelton, ninety miles away.

The unit was a pit stop for stressed out men waiting to go nowhere good. Kennedy spent five weeks there. "Everybody there was trying to prove themselves and there's just a lot of trouble," he says. Not long after he got there, he saw a corrections officer shouting into an inmate's face.

"The next thing you know the guard put his finger in the guy's face and the guy stepped back away from him. And the guard attacked him and three other guards attacked him on top of that, and they beat the shit out of that guy for no reason. He did not pose a physical threat. And I thought, oh boy, I've got some bad-attitude cops to deal with."

Kennedy did time in five prisons over nine years, spending no more than two years in each. The first was Washington State Penitentiary—commonly known as Walla Walla, after the town it's in—a two-thousand-inmate facility surrounded by wheat fields, and the site of the state's death row.

When he got there, an officer handed him a bedroll and ordered him to his cell. As he made his bed, someone behind him growled, "What the hell are you doing here?" Kennedy spun around with his fists raised—and cracked a wide smile. His cellie turned out to be Scott Booth, a buddy from Castle Rock High School, who was doing time for vehicular manslaughter. Scott had not heard about Kennedy's case, and after getting the rundown said, "There's no way you done that. Absolutely not."

Kennedy couldn't believe his good luck, running into Scott on his first day at Walla Walla. So it was downright shocking when he ran into another old buddy the same day. Kennedy was on his way to the prison office to get a pencil and some paper when someone leapt on him. "I go to stomp on him and I realize it's my friend Jeff Fouch," he says. "I picked him up off the ground and am like, 'Wow this is crazy.'" Jeff was in prison because six years earlier he beat to death a pervert who touched his little brother. And like Scott, Jeff had no doubt that Kennedy was innocent.

Old friends were a precious commodity for a guy locked up for child rape—a "funny beef," as inmates called those kinds of convicts. Sometimes guys would ask Kennedy what he was in for, already knowing the answer but just wanting to hear Kennedy say it. He had a stock answer, "First-degree assault. Want to try it?"

Some guys would steal his commissary just to mess with him. Or, Kennedy says, "they'd run their little pussy mouths" as he walked by, hollering, "Rape!" or "Rapo!" Sometimes they'd yell out, "ChiMo!"—a prison abbreviation for child molester. Sometimes gang leaders would launch "missiles" at him—young inmates who'd attack funny beefs as part of gang initiation.

"Every time they did it, it just reminded me of my daughter lying about me. It just brought up that burden," Kennedy says.

Ironically, the first time Kennedy ever flew in an airplane was as a convict. A year into Walla Walla he boarded a ramshackle jet to fly twelve-hundred miles to Crowley County Correctional Facility in Olney Springs, Colorado.

"I tried to enjoy it, the takeoff, the thrust of power, the lifting in the air," he says. "The little bit of pleasure only lasted a couple minutes."

He got the window seat just behind the wing, which jiggled up and down like it was going to rip right off. "I wished the plane would crash," Kennedy says, laughing. "At the time, it seemed like my only hope because I was getting yanked away from my family and friends."

The flight crew served each inmate a turkey sub with vegetables, two cookies, a banana, and some orange juice. "The thing about that is when inmates are in transport, they don't want to eat because they'll have to go to bathroom. When you've got the other guys cuffed to you, they're not happy about it."

So Kennedy just held it in and spaced out on the wonder of seeing clouds from above. "I kind of let my mind go back to my childhood, when I used to ride with my dad in the log truck. We'd go up the mountains and be above the clouds and above the fog coming in, and I looked down on it, down in the valley. It was pretty neat. I just kind of reverted my mind back to those memories, so I wouldn't focus on what was bothering me."

Getting out of prison was a relative molehill compared to the real challenge: forgiving Cassandra. For a long time, he couldn't even begin that climb. So he put his mind toward other things like letter writing, taking college correspondence courses, working prison jobs, and exercising.

To fight off the crippling isolation that a funny beef suffers, particularly for the six years Kennedy was in out-of-state prisons and got not one visitor, he wrote about thirty letters a week—to his parents, stepdad, ex-girlfriend, aunts, uncles, cousins, even strangers he found on Christian pen pal lists. It felt good pouring his heart out to regular folks on the outside, innocent people, like him. He even "dated" one of his Christian pen pals for a couple years, a woman named Lori, until she broke up with him in one of her letters.

He took a variety of correspondence courses that included roofing and siding, and entrepreneurial science—anything he thought might be useful when he got out. He also took an anger management course and a course that earned him certification as a relaxation therapist. That last one might have been the most valuable investment he ever made in prison. "I learned to monitor my own anxiety levels by reading my pulse and my tone of voice, and relieving that stress before it affected my body. I think prisons should make everyone take that course."

Also soothing to Kennedy's nerves was beading—making earrings, necklaces, and pouches out of tiny beads that he'd then sell to other inmates or send to relatives as gifts. "I never really set goals in my life until after I got locked up," Kennedy says. "I started hearing some talk from a preacher man about setting goals, so I figured I'm gonna try this out, have four pairs of earrings done by end of the day. I'd mess up, but instead of getting angry, I'd just get up and walk around the dayroom a couple times and go back to it. I would reach that goal of four pairs of earrings. I learned patience and I learned accomplishment. It just kept me peaceful."

Kennedy's confidence grew as he climbed the prison employment ladder, working on maintenance crews and construction crews, scrubbing pots in the kitchen, and washing laundry, until eventually he landed the most

coveted job of all: Captain's Crew. This meant doing various grunt work for the corrections captain in charge, like
carting stuff around or setting up rooms for events—but
only for a few hours a day, and then getting paid to relax
and let the clock run.

The Captain's Crew members were chummy with officers in a way regular inmates weren't. "Sometimes guards
dropped a bag of smoked salmon out of their lunch bag
when they were walking by you and keep on walking.
You'd just say, 'Oh, look what I found,' and eat it real quick."
Kennedy even shared his secret deer jerky recipe with one
of the guards. "Two weeks later he brought in his version
of it. It was pretty good."

I forgive you, Cassandra. I forgive you, Cassandra.
Kennedy chanted the words every day, over and over,
as if in prayer. He said them before he went to sleep. He
said them while scrubbing pots and pans, exercising in
the rec yard, folding laundry. Kennedy had been praying
since he was a teenager, but had only really found Jesus
when he quit drinking and knew he couldn't stay sober
without help from a higher power.

For five years he kept chanting those words as if they
were true. And as life regulated and the trauma faded, he
started believing them.

And then they were true.

"That's my little girl," he says. "If I hold that bitterness,
if I don't forgive, it's just gonna eat me up."

Now he prayed for something else: that Cassandra
would come forth and tell the truth, and free her father
from bondage.

Kennedy hated everything about the appeal process.
Just getting into the law library was difficult because it

was only open during odd hours. And doing the research meant deciphering impossibly dense legalese. He'd fill out the paperwork in a way he hoped was half-competent, and send it off—only to receive a rejection many months later.

Then he'd just start over.

"It was harder and harder to deal with, causing more stress in my life every time I got a response back from the court or from the prosecution. It would just really make me angry, them not saying, 'OK, we'll free the man.' I didn't want that anger. I didn't want it with me."

The frustration was compounded by a personal tragedy—the death of his ex-girlfriend Tammy. Even though they'd broken up, she kept writing regularly and her supportive letters meant a lot to him. Tammy had been in a car wreck two years earlier that paralyzed her from the neck down. She was starting to improve, even move her arms a little. And then suddenly her body quit on her.

After several years of representing himself, Kennedy got one more rejection letter from the court and decided it would be his last. He doesn't remember specifically what the letter said or from which court it came. He just remembers his pulse racing and his fist crushing the paper. "I knew I was going to explode if I kept this up, and that's not a pretty sight. People get hurt when I do that; they get hurt really bad."

So he gave it up to the Lord.

"Here you go, Father, please take this legal work, and make the truth come forth so that I be set free," he said. "I'm not gonna fight it no more."

In 2005, Kennedy boarded another plane and flew to Prairie Correctional Facility in Appleton, Minnesota—1,700 miles from home. For whatever reason, his funny beef status made him a bigger target there than anywhere before.

Gangsters attacked him so often that Kennedy's knuckles were constantly scuffed from fighting back.

One time, after leaving a young missile unconscious on the floor, Kennedy walked up to the table where the gang leaders were sitting. "Why don't you have enough balls to send a group of the well-seasoned veterans my way, instead of sending boys along and scratching my knuckles?" he said.

A few days later, Kennedy was playing guitar in his cell when six evil-looking guys charged through the doorway. Kennedy hurled the guitar at the one in front, then pummeled his face, wrecking his lip and cheekbone. A brawl ensued with bodies bouncing off the cell walls. When it was all done, Kennedy went to the hole for twenty days as punishment for the face shot.

Once, an inmate shoved him down a flight of stairs. He toppled down twenty steps and tore up his knee, banged his head and pulled muscles in his back. He'd been carrying a folder of papers and his Brother typewriter, and the papers scattered everywhere. The typewriter was the only thing that came out of it unscathed.

Another time, Kennedy was writing a letter when an ugly guy named Gary sat down across from him. "I think you're a piece of shit for doing what you did," Gary said, referring to his funny beef.

Kennedy put down his pencil. "Listen, Gary," he said, "I'll give you this opportunity to walk away. Otherwise, I'll hurt you really bad because you're a big dude and I won't fuck around. So you need to go."

"Well, you ain't going to do nothing about it," Gary retorted. "You're a coward. A piece of shit."

A short time later, Gary was in his cell when Kennedy walked in holding a jug of baby powder and a gym sock with a bar of soap in the toe.

"Get up, bitch," Kennedy ordered. Gary obliged. Kennedy threw baby powder in Gary's face, blinding and choking him. Then he whacked him hard with the sock. Gary went down and Kennedy kicked him in the head. Then he swung the bar of soap at him over and over as fast as he could. An inmate named Tiger pulled Kennedy away before he could do more damage. The attack got Kennedy six months in the hole.

Later on he found out Gary was locked up for child molestation. Kennedy was not surprised. "A lot of the guys that ran around all tough, shaving their heads and getting tattoos and calling people rapos, were guilty of it themselves," he says.

"I learned that he who is first to accuse is guilty himself."

The week before Thanksgiving 2009, Kennedy got on a plane for the third time, to fly from Minnesota to Monroe Correctional Complex in Monroe, Washington. He was there for about a year before he went to Stafford Creek Corrections Center in Aberdeen, only about one hundred miles from home.

Being closer to home didn't lighten the expression on the face that greeted him in the mirror every morning. "I would see the desperation in my eyes, this absolute look of despair, like, *What am I going to do? I don't know what to do.* Because I knew I was innocent in that prison."

So it was startling one day to see that very same look on the face of another man who walked into the rec room.

"I see this guy come walking in the unit and he stopped and took a look around," he says. "I do the same thing, get the feel of the room before I go in. I said, 'Hmm, he has that kind of character about him'. Then he looked in my eyes and I seen that same look of desperation, and my guts told me he was in prison for the same reason that I was."

That inmate's name was Shawn, and he'd been convicted of raping his son. After reviewing his case, Kennedy
decided without a doubt that Shawn was innocent. They
became cellies and bonded like brothers.

One nasty, grey day in January 2012, Shawn had just
come back from a workout and was sitting on his bunk
waiting for the showers to open up when Kennedy walked
in. Something wasn't right with Kennedy; he was normally
very fidgety, but now he was still as a rock.

"Thomas, you OK?" Shawn asked.

Kennedy looked at his friend. "Shawn, I think I'm
going home."

The day had started innocuously enough. Shawn had
asked him if he wanted to come outside to work out,
but the weather was too cold and wet. Instead, Kennedy
worked on a gift he was making for his cousin Kaylee-
na—a black and gold seed-bead choker necklace with
tiger eye gemstones dangling from it. After a while, his
butt started to hurt from sitting on his paper-plate-sized
stool, so he got up and went to the dayroom to stretch out.

Then he called his mom. Her voice sounded strange.

"Are you sitting down?" she asked him.

"Yeah, Momma, I'm sitting down. What you got to say?"

"You know the thing you've been praying for? Well,
it happened."

Kennedy didn't know what she was talking about. He
prayed for all kinds of things.

"You know, that thing that's been bugging you for a
while," his mother said.

"No, Mom, I'm not catching on with what you're saying,"
Kennedy said—and then suddenly he caught on. And he
was glad his mother had told him to sit down.

Cassandra has come forth and told the truth.

Kennedy was silent for a good minute. His mother grew worried.

"Thomas, did you pass out?" she asked.

That made Kennedy laugh, and then hosannas rushed from his lips. "Praise Jesus, hallelujah," he cried. "Thank you, God. Thank you for answering my prayers."

Cassandra's life had taken a downward turn after her father went to prison. She started having troubles at school and was expelled after sending her teacher a letter threatening to take a gun and shoot the place up.

She did make it into high school, but only lasted until her junior year and dropped out. She became addicted to pills and meth, and amassed a string of convictions for burglary and theft. At twenty-three she sought help at a Christian addiction treatment center called Mountain Ministries, in the town of Kelso, just across the Cowlitz River from Longview.

A few months later, on January 23, 2012, she called Longview police and said she wanted to talk about her father's case. Three days later, Cassandra sat down with detectives and said, "I did a horrible thing."[2] She'd accused her father of raping her to get back at him for drinking and smoking pot and being absent from her life. "I wanted him to love me, and I didn't think he did at that time," she told the stunned cops. "He wasn't showing up. I wanted him away so he would stop hurting me."

So she came up with the rape accusation after a friend's father got locked up for a sex crime. "I took my own vengeance," she said. But she hadn't predicted the severity of the outcome. "I just thought he would go away, you know, go to jail for a little bit, be out of my life," she said.

For years, Cassandra dulled her guilt by drinking and drugging. But now she was ready to free her father—and herself. "It's not OK to sit and be locked in this horrible place for something you didn't do. It's just not right," she said. "I just want him to be out and freed...I will be free on the inside."

Kennedy's nerves were on fire.

Prison had become home; now he was facing the prospect of leaving it to face a hostile new world all alone. Even worse was the paranoia that he *wouldn't* get out. The voice in his head taunted him. *They're not gonna let me out. They're gonna just keep screwing me. They've screwed me all this time.*

He'd go to the gym, the yard, and the library. He'd do some paperwork, have lunch, and work his afternoon job cleaning a bathroom—getting it so sparkling that officers from other units would come use it.

And, to himself, he'd praise Cassandra: *Good girl, Cassandra. You're coming forth and telling the truth. Good girl.*

A few weeks after his mother broke the good news to him, a corrections officer named McNew approached him and said, "Kennedy, it's been nice knowing you."

Kennedy asked him what he meant by that.

"You're going to court," McNew said. "Your name's on the papers on the sergeant's desk."

"Don't fuck with me, McNew," Kennedy said. The officer swore he wasn't.

"Well, Mr. McNew," Kennedy said with a wide grin, "under different circumstances I'd give you a handshake and a big hug. It's been a pleasure knowing you. You're a hell of a good man."

The next day, Kennedy went to Cowlitz County Court. His lawyer Terry Mulligan, director of the Cowlitz County Office of Public Defense, filed for a new trial. Soon after, prosecutor Susie Baur wrote a letter to Superior Court

Justice Stephen Warning saying she was made aware of new, credible material evidence that potentially made it likely that Kennedy was innocent.

Kennedy sat in the county jail across the street from the courthouse for thirty-six days, a period he describes as overwhelmingly joyful and extremely horrible. "I hadn't had time to prepare my mind to be out in the free world," he says. "I was scared for so many reasons. I feared for my life. I was scared about being around people. I was scared about being around kids, about somebody else lying about me again. I was scared that I would never get a job again.

"When a guy gets exonerated from prison, it's no small affair, especially in the small local area he's from. There's people that say, 'Man, that's just horrible you spent nine years in prison. I'm sorry to hear that.' And there's some people who say, 'Well you spent nine years in prison so you did *something.*'"

On March 26, 2012, Kennedy experienced a walloping déjà vu as he sat in a courtroom watching Cassandra testify about him again. She tearfully told the packed court that she'd made up the rape story to make her father go away, because of his drinking and pot-smoking habit. She explained that her genital trauma from that time had actually been caused by a boy she'd messed around with in second grade. The boy in question was also in court that day and testified to the same.

Kennedy listened in a fog, his mind repeating the same phrase it had repeated the last time he and his daughter squared off in court. *This can't be happening. This can't be happening.* But the voice uttering those words was now joyful.

"That day, I got to have closure on the matter, whether I was set free or not," he says. "I got to see my daughter point at me on that stand and say, 'It wasn't him.' Hearing her say that…I'd been praying for that specific thing all those years."

Judge Warning apologized to Kennedy for the injustice that was done to him. He asked the corrections officers to process the exoneree speedily. Kennedy was taken back across the street to his cell, where he lay his head on his pillow and took a nap.

He woke a couple hours later to a tapping on the bars.

"Roll 'em up," the officer said. "You're going home."

Stuffy's II Restaurant in Longview prides itself in its astronomical portions—things like six-pound cinnamon rolls and the "Almost a Dozen Egg Omelet" (finish it in forty-five minutes and you get your choice of shirt or hat, plus your picture on the hall of fame).

Since his first day in prison, Kennedy had been dreaming of Stuffy's biscuits and gravy. So his family took him to the restaurant for his first stop out of prison, and he wolfed down two giant biscuits served on a sixteen-inch pizza platter, and when he was done he started picking off his mother's and grandson Garrett's plates. He ate until his gut could hold no more. "It was exactly as I remembered it," he says.

The family all went to Kennedy's mother's house after that, where the festivities continued as family and friends stopped by to offer congratulations. When it got too overwhelming, Kennedy went to the Cowlitz River and soaked his feet in the water for a couple of hours.

In prison, Kennedy had made a checklist of all the things he would do when he got out—get his driver's license, car insurance, a job, his own place. Over time, most of the items on that list would be checked off. But one would have a permanent star next to it instead of a check. "Be proactive in Garrett's life," was the item.

"It's to remind me that that's a goal that needs to be reached every day, all the time," Kennedy says.

When Kennedy's story hit newsstands, online vitriol toward Cassandra followed. Reddit and other social media sites were loaded with demands that Cassandra be prosecuted for what she did to her father. An April 8, 2012, an editorial in the *Longview Daily News* called it "the sort of case almost designed to generate outrage," adding, "a 'Get Out of Jail Free' card for Cassandra Kennedy seems inherently unjust."

But, the editorial acknowledged, the statute of limitations was up, so prosecuting Cassandra was impossible. Even if it had been possible, it would have been ethically questionable to prosecute a woman who'd committed a crime as a child. And doing so could discourage others who'd sent people to prison for false claims from coming forward and telling the truth.

"Regardless of whether or not it 'feels right,'" the editorial concluded, "the decision not to attempt prosecution was the only defensible and appropriate course of action."

On Easter Sunday 2012, Kennedy bought a bouquet of daffodils from a Safeway supermarket and drove to the Seventh Day Adventist Church in the town of Lexington. He waited outside the church until he saw her. They'd planned this meeting in advance, but she looked terrified just the same.

"I love you, Princess," he said, and handed Cassandra the bouquet. Her face lit up and they embraced.

"I love you too, Dad," she said. "But I don't like being called that no more. I'm grown up."

"You'll always be my princess," Kennedy said.

They sat down to a buffet breakfast at the church and caught up a little on each other's lives. Cassandra told her father about her recovery at Mountain Ministries and her recent missionary trip to Mexico. Kennedy told her about prison life. They talked about their plans for the future. Kennedy felt at ease breaking bread with his daughter, but Cassandra's anxiety was radiating out of her.

"Don't worry about what happened," he told her. "I was never mad at you. I feel I don't even have to forgive you because I never was mad at you."

After breakfast, they prayed and then listened to the pastor's sermon. Then Cassandra walked her father to the parking lot, where they hugged once more before Kennedy drove away. They saw each other nearly every other day after that, sometimes at Bible study, sometimes at each other's homes.

Then they went on TV with Katie Couric and Cassandra had her meltdown at the airport. After that, Kennedy kept his distance whenever he felt tension with his daughter. But one day he couldn't walk away because they were in his truck on Interstate 5, fighting about Kennedy's temporary custody arrangement for Garrett while the boy's mother, Marlena, served jail time for drug possession.

"All you're trying to do is take Garrett away from your daughter," Cassandra said.

"Goddamnit, I want the best for him," Kennedy said. "I don't want him in a foster home somewhere. If I'm taking care of him and watching him, I know that he's safe."

Things escalated, and then Cassandra said the thing Kennedy swore he'd never let her say again. "You know what? I'm gonna put you back in prison. I'm not gonna do it myself this time, but I'll have someone else do it."

Kennedy wanted to kick her out of his truck, right there on the highway. But he made it the last few miles and when he pulled up to her place, she got out and slammed the door.

He didn't speak to her for a long time after that, even when she texted him to say she was pregnant. "It's my kid," he says. "I love her. I'm scared to death of being alone with her and what have you. If we have to keep it at a long distance relationship then I'm gonna do that. I have to feel safe, period."

"You see that big fish jump right over there, Garrett? Big old steelhead jumped right out of the water. It's gone now. It just jumped out and got back in."

It's sixty degrees on an early-April afternoon, and Kennedy and Garrett are on the banks of the Cowlitz River. The clear sky is a treat today, because it's been overcast and rainy for days.

Not that a little rain ever bothered a native Washingtonian.

The Cowlitz River is stunningly beautiful, lined with trees and mountains all along its hundred-and-five-mile span. It branches off from the mighty Columbia River and channels melted snow from as high as Mount St. Helens to the Pacific Ocean.

Kennedy likes to come here with Garrett, a hazel-eyed, blond-haired boy, who, like his grandpa, prefers work boots to sneakers. And while Garrett runs along the bank and makes mud pies, Kennedy likes to look out at God's bounty and pray. "I've learned to dearly appreciate moments like this," he says. "I would sit in prison and remember moments like this and worry about never being able to experience them again. And by God's grace, I am here."

"I'm hungry," Garrett tells his grampa in a voice as sweet as Bambi's.

"There's a sandwich up in the pickup," Kennedy says.

In an hour or so, when the temperature drops, Kennedy and Garrett will get in the truck and head back to their trailer in nearby Castle Rock.

When Kennedy got out of prison, he immediately set out looking for a job. He found one after three weeks, doing maintenance for a slumlord for eight bucks an hour. Then he got his driver's license and bought a pickup truck, which he used to haul wooden pallets and sell them to factories that either reused them or ground them into mulch.

The pallet business was a fickle one. A good day brought in one hundred dollars in profits and a bad day got him nothing but wasted gas. He got a job maintaining the campground where he lives, but that only netted him one hundred eighty dollars a week.

What else could he do? He tried enrolling as a student on the online University of Phoenix, but found the enrollment process insurmountably complicated. "The Internet just frustrates me," he says. "You gotta do all this different shit to accomplish one thing. And you got to provide so much information. At first, I would give them information and then my email would just get flooded with crap."

Even setting up a Netflix account for Garrett to watch cartoons was a lost cause. "I tried for a couple hours to do it and I couldn't get through it. I don't even know how to use a credit card on the Internet. I tried twice and it pissed me off, and I haven't done it since. It's way too frustrating to deal with."

In 2014, the state agreed to pay up $472,000 in restitution. "They didn't really oppose it none," he says. "They asked some questions and we answered them and they said, 'We concede on the order.'"

"I gave praise and thanks to God because he deserves all credit."

Kennedy plans to put the money toward starting businesses in pallets, storage, and even some real estate. "I'm going to be happy because I know I will have played a big part in securing my grandson's future and my kids' future and help their lives get better," he says.

It starts to rain, but Kennedy and Garrett pay it no mind. It only rains for a little while anyway. And when it clears, Kennedy spots something that even a jaded Pacific Northwesterner like himself can't help but appreciate.

"There is a rainbow on the bank right on the other side of the river," he shouts to his grandson, who's still making mud pies by the banks. Garrett looks up and admires the sight for a moment and goes back to his pies.

Kennedy starts talking about the panic attacks he gets sometimes, thinking someone might lie about him again and send him to prison. "What's Garrett gonna do if he comes home from school and finds out Papa's in jail?" he asks. "How will that affect him? There's times I don't even leave the trailer because I'm afraid something's gonna happen."

As Kennedy mulls life's uncertainties, Garrett waddles up with a big mud pie that's dripping through his fingers. "Here's your birthday cake," Garrett says.

Kennedy's voice, tense a moment ago, is now sweet. "Thank you, buddy," he says "A mud cake with a candlestick in it!"

"Happy birthday to you, happy birthday to you," Garrett sings. Then he tells his grampa to make a wish.

"I just did," Kennedy says, and blows out the candle.

Chapter 8

KERRY PORTER
Kentucky, 13 Years

When Kerry Porter was in lockup, he used to sit on the toilet for so long that when he'd finally get up, it would take a good half hour before his legs got full circulation back.

The other inmates thought he must have had the worst case of constipation in Northpoint.

Which would have been quite a feat, given how often guys got clogged pipes from prison chow—about which they used to say, "It only makes a turd. It don't do nothing effective for you."

But Porter wasn't on the shitter to shit; he was there to get work done. For three hours straight he'd perch his ass on the can with a fat volume of case law on his lap, underlining sentences, taking notes in the margins, strategizing. It was one of the few really quiet places he could work.

And work is all he did, eighteen hours a day, every day, for the singular purpose of proving he didn't shoot a man dead at a truck stop in Louisville.

"I played ping pong maybe forty times the whole time I was locked up," he says. "I probably played chess I doubt twenty times—and I really enjoy chess. I enjoy the hell out of ping pong. And I enjoy the hell out of dominoes.

And I played dominoes maybe a hundred times, mainly because we was on lockdown a whole lot and I couldn't get to the law library. And even playing dominoes, I'm still working on my case in my head.

"I slept with paperwork under my pillow in case I woke up in the middle of the night and had a thought, and sometimes the papers fell out and landed on my cellie's head. This happened like five times. We almost got into fights over that."

Prison rules said each inmate could possess two cubic feet of legal work; Porter had more than double that, stored away under his bed and in laundry bags. The officers nicknamed him "Fire Hazard."

One day a captain came over and told Porter he'd personally throw out his papers if Porter didn't do it himself.

"That's my life, man," Porter said.

"I don't give a damn," the captain said. "If when I come back here this shit ain't gone, I'm gonna throw it in the garbage."

Porter blew his top. "Motherfucker!" he shouted, "If you touch my legal work–" And with that, two officers grabbed him and tossed him in the hole for ten days.

Moments like that could put a yoke on Porter, slow down his momentum, stress him out, and hurt his confidence. "You're dealing with emotions," he says. "You're dealing with—oh man, failure on a regular basis. You're dealing with anxiety. You're dealing with inmates and guards criticizing you, saying, 'You ain't never getting out of here. Admit you did it.'"

Porter would shake off the words like George Foreman would shake off an uppercut to the jaw. He had to, because it's only worth living behind bars if you're hell-bent on getting out.

Kerry Porter always had a terrific work ethic, but mostly for the wrong kind of work.

As a teenager, he found out how easy it was to steal cars. He mostly stuck with GMs—Regals, Monte Carlos, Cadillacs, Cutlasses, El Caminos, Camaros, you name it—because they were the easiest to jack. At first, he hot-wired just to joyride. But after getting hooked on crack in his twenties, his actual occupation, bricklaying, wasn't bringing in enough green. Auto theft became his main source of revenue. He was damned good at it, stealing an estimated seven hundred cars over two decades.

"I was a one-man auto ring," says Porter, a light-skinned black man with doe-like eyes and a hard Kentucky drawl. "During the peak of my addiction, it was really bad, probably ten a week. I think the max I stole was like four cars in one night."

He'd drive the cars out to the swampy backwoods of his hometown of Newburg, Kentucky, a suburb of Louisville. He'd strip out the good stuff first, the rims, the radios, the kicker boxes, and sell it out of his pickup truck to drug dealers.

When Porter got bold in his addiction, he would just drive the cars right into the parking lot of his apartment complex and gut them right there in the open. "God has some type of plan because I don't see how I wasn't killed during these car thefts," he says. "I was almost shot several times."

He remembers one time in particular when, while wasted, he broke into an '85 El Dorado in the parking lot of a Holiday Inn. "I was going to take the radio out of there and all the goods and sell them real quick. And before I could do that, a guy reached in and started choking me." Then another guy appeared, and Porter predicted death coming his way real soon. So he pulled out his pink-handled chrome .25 and both guys started running. "I got out of the car and shot in the air just to give me a little room," he says. "And I got away. That was a close call—if the guy had had a knife he could have cut my throat."

But that's how Porter rolled, putting his life at risk to feed the insatiable monster. His son little Kerry was just two when Porter got hooked on drugs, and it haunts him to this day knowing he put his addiction above his little boy. "I think all he wanted was for me to be the type of father I was supposed to be," he says.

Porter was one of those lowlifes who gets arrested again and again and again—three dozen times, in his case—and never learns. He did short stints in jail for auto theft, gun possession, drug possession, and failing to pay child support after splitting with little Kerry's mom Cecilia.

So the day cops questioned him about the murder of Tyrone Camp, Porter had as much credibility as the boy who cried wolf.

In 1996, sixty-eight people were murdered in Louisville, a record high. The last to go was a nice-enough guy named Tyrone Camp, a thirty-five-year-old truck driver who was warming up his rig one frigid morning, two days after Christmas, when someone crept up and shot him in the head and back. The gunman left behind a silencer made of rolled-up carpet.

There had been only one witness, another trucker named Kenneth Brown, who told cops he couldn't identify the gunman. It had been pitch black out, save for the gleam from Brown's headlights, and he'd only seen the side of the killer's face from about twenty feet away.

But a few weeks later, the dead man's twin brother Jerome showed Brown a photo of Kerry Porter and asked him if Porter was the killer. Jerome suspected as much because Tyrone Camp's wife Cecilia was Porter's ex-girl-friend and the mother of Porter's child. Jerome thought maybe Porter had gotten so jealous—especially seeing Camp raising little Kerry—that he'd shot him.

Brown studied the photo and nodded. Porter was the man who'd killed Tyrone Camp, he said. Two days later, Brown went to the cops and picked out Porter's snapshot from a photo lineup.

Not long before the murder, Porter had wrapped up a sixteen-month prison stint for auto theft. Once out, he went right back to his old habits, smoking crack—as much as a quarter ounce a day—and stealing cars. Two months out of prison, he predictably got busted again, this time for stealing cars and scrap metal.

At his January 1997 court appearance for that crime, a police officer approached Porter and said he wanted to interview him as part of an investigation into Tyrone Camp's murder. Porter obliged, and during questioning was asked his location the morning of Camp's murder.

Porter said he'd been at his girlfriend Donna's place.

He would later realize that was incorrect. Donna had been in a drug treatment program at the time of the murder, and Porter had been on his sister's couch, sleep-ing off a crack hangover. The mistake came from Porter's being high during the interview, and it did him no favors during the police investigation later on.

Later that month, he appeared in court again for the auto theft and scrap metal charges—and to his shock, the judge ordered him locked up on $110,000 bond. He was hauled away to Community Correctional Center in Louisville. "I left the street on January 28, 1997," he says, "and didn't see the streets again for fourteen years, ten months, and twenty-one days."

In February 1997, Porter was indicted for murdering Tyrone Camp. He was floored when he read through the court papers. "When I seen my name beside the words *life sentence* and all this crazy stuff, I know it's a frame up and they're coming at me way too hard."

What he read included a statement from a jailhouse snitch named Greg Gully, who had shared a cell with Porter at CCC and later told authorities Porter had confessed to the killing. There was also a statement from an old friend Marcus Pendergrast, who told police that a month before the murder Porter was at a barbecue and saw his ex with her new husband Tyrone Camp, laughing away. Porter supposedly became incensed, muttering, "I am going to kill him. I am going to kill him."[1]

Lies! But how would a jury know that? Porter, already feeling defeated, lay down in his cell and slept on and off for a week. "Every time I woke up, I had this horrible thought that this is the real deal here. To make things worse, my mother was completely traumatized. She was trying to sell her house to get a good lawyer at good law firm to defend me. Everybody's panicking because it's a murder case. It was all off balance because we'd never dealt with something of this nature before."

That summer, Porter pleaded guilty to auto theft and burglary in exchange for a five-year sentence, and was shipped to Northpoint Training Center, a former psychiatric hospital some eighty miles southwest of Louisville. He was now property of the state of Kentucky—but never mind that. With a murder trial on the horizon, Porter threw himself into his homework.

He studied case law on eyewitness identification, particularly *Neil v. Biggers*, the landmark 1972 Supreme Court decision that established legal criteria for eyewitness reliability. He worked on finding ways to discredit other kinds of "witnesses," like Greg Gully and Marcus Pendergrast. He tried to enter into evidence that a hoodlum named Juan Leotis Sanders was screwing around with Tyrone Camp's wife Cecilia, and together they had conspired to kill Camp and collect on his $150,000 life insurance policy. He learned that police were missing the key piece of evidence, the murder weapon.

"I'm working in the law library and I'm finding out all of these things about my case," he says. "I'm finding out that they don't have this and can't prove that. I'm finding out that my case is no more than a circumstantial one."

Yet he knew that acquittal boiled down to jurors taking his word over jailhouse snitch Greg Gully's.

"I knew I was in for a hell of a battle."

Porter's marathon effort was briefly sidetracked by a strange and terrible incident in which he found himself in court once again—to testify against a corrections officer whom he'd witnessed stomping an inmate to death.

On January 6, 1998, Porter saw in the cell across from him a group of officers surrounding inmate Adrian Reynolds, who had been arrested six days earlier for allegedly beating up his girlfriend. Porter would later testify that he watched in horror as Officer Timothy Barnes stomped Reynolds's head bloody with his boot.

"I called it, Murder in Cell Six," Porter says. "They busted his head wide open again and dragged him out of there in handcuffs. On the way out his head bumped against the wall and all his blood was on the wall. It was a horrible, horrible thing to see."

Porter went to trial eighteen months after he got thrown in jail on the burglary charges. A day before the trial began, the eyewitness Kenneth Brown met with prosecutors and told them that he was no longer certain he'd identified the right man in the photo lineup. He asked to see the photos again. He would go on to testify at the five-day trial that Porter was the gunman.

Prosecutors presented Porter as a jilted lover, infuriated that Camp had not only married his ex, but was helping raise little Kerry. "He hated that Tyrone Camp had taken his place, and he hated Tyrone Camp," Prosecutor McKay Chauvin said in his opening statement.[2]

The commonwealth's star witness Greg Gully stated he and Porter had been watching an episode of *Baywatch* when Porter said he'd killed Camp. Marcus Pendergrast testified about Porter's threat against Camp at the barbecue a month before the murder.

Prosecutors highlighted Porter's failure to provide a proper alibi when he was questioned after the shooting. To counter that, Porter's sister and niece testified he was with them when Camp was killed.

Porter's lawyer tried to tilt the jury's attention off Porter and onto Juan Leotis Sanders, whom she contended killed Camp to cash in on his life insurance policy. (Seven months later, Sanders would get seventeen years behind bars for shooting three people, killing one.)

In the thick of these proceedings, Porter spoke to little Kerry for the last time. It was a brief conversation. The boy walked into the courtroom with his aunt and a cousin and sat down in the back row.

Porter turned to looked at his son and said, "How you doing, little Kerry?"

"Hi, Daddy," little Kerry said.

And that's the last image Porter has of his boy to this day. "Never in my wildest dreams did I know that that would be the last time so far that I'd spoken to him," he says.

It took the jury forty minutes to deliberate. When the verdict came back, Porter was ready for it.

"I took it on the chin because I already saw where this case was going, how it was gonna play out," he says. "If it was a fight, it was four people against a crippled kid. That's the analogy that I always use. That's how bad it was."

Prior acceptance of his fate helped. He could skip the shock and mourning stages and just get straight to work. Porter called his mother as soon as he could. She broke down sobbing. "Listen, Ma," he said, "you told me when you're in a fight, ain't no time to cry. You just start swinging. This is what I need from you." He started listing things like his typewriter and the trial tapes.

"I didn't care about a TV, Walkman, or any of that comfort-type of stuff," he says today. "All I wanted was to fight my case."

He was sentenced to sixty years. A jailbird pal told Porter it would take seven or eight years to overturn his case. "I was ready to fight him just for saying that—and that was a best friend of mine," Porter says. "I said, 'Why you say something like that? I'll be out in three years.' Then it kind of settled in my mind that, man, this guy was telling me the truth. So I made up my mind that I'm gonna do eight years."

That turned out to be a lowball estimation, too, but Porter hustled like the goal was reachable. He enrolled in a class to become a legal aid and learned about open records and how to obtain them from the police department, the court clerk's office, the medical examiner, and even the FBI. To save money mailing in all those requests, Porter made his own envelopes out of typewriter paper, and recycled stamps by rubbing out the postmarks with underarm deodorant.

He'd sign each letter as "The Fall Guy" or "The Innocent One."

It was adrenaline to Porter's fragile morale every time he received a requested document—like the one that said Juan Leotis Sanders and Cecilia Camp were briefly investigated for the murder. Or the one that said Marcus Pendergrast, who had testified against Porter, was a convicted felon. "I paraded these documents to case workers, because everybody knew that this guy's been working on his case five years, eight years, ten years, and he ain't got out yet. Yeah, I ain't got out yet, you're dead right. But one day, man, real soon I'll have enough documents to present to the court that they'll have no choice but to give me a new trial."

Kerry Porter lived and breathed criminal law. Casual conversations with inmates and officers always revolved around his case or someone else's. When he watched the tube it was always the news. When he read the newspaper, he'd keep an eye out for anything having to do with government corruption. And when he found a story highlighting police or prosecutorial screwups like the Duke lacrosse rape case or the Memphis Four or the Central Park Five, he'd tear the clipping out and save it.

As for day-to-day life in the clink, the less attention Porter gave it, the better.

"The food is beyond horrible," he says. "It's barely edible. One time they served us chicken that had been badly spoiled. They'd washed it, put vinegar and Worcestershire sauce on it, fried it, and served it to us. I got food poisoning, and that was the worst thing ever. You actually want to die when you get this."

The food was so famously bad at Northpoint that in 2009, after Porter had been transferred out, inmates rioted and set fires that destroyed buildings and caused several injuries. Investigators would pin the riot on anger over a lockdown, but it was common knowledge that the food situation fueled the anger.

The showers were overcrowded and the hot water often didn't work. But that wasn't the worst of it: "The water would stop up," Porter says. "Guys would masturbate in the shower, shit and piss in the shower, have sex in the shower. Your everyday thing was, do I really have to deal with this? Hear this, see this, smell this?

"Then you got the guards acting crazy, searching you every time, frisking you every search. I gotta put up with this? They want to touch your nuts and your thing. That's mentally hard on you; every day you're gonna get touched by a guard."

Or worse, getting told by a wiseass guard or inmate, "You're never getting out of here, so quit wasting your time trying—because you're a killer, just like everybody else."

Sometimes he'd get spit at or knocked around by guys who assumed Porter killed Tyrone Camp. The murder would, in itself, have been cool or even admirable to them, except he supposedly did it out of jealousy—not considered a noble motive in prison circles. Porter threw a punch at one of these guys once, and promptly got the piss beaten out of him. "He pounded me against everything in the TV room," he says. "He whupped me pretty good. That fight blacked my eye and my jaw seemed looser than before. But no bones broken."

For a few stretches, Porter endured the ultimate indignity of living in the same facility as Juan Leotis Sanders, the hoodlum who'd been suspected but never charged in the killing of Tyrone Camp. For one awful set of months, Porter had to share a block with Sanders, using the same showers, receiving mail from the same deliverer, using the same phones. "That was a horrible experience. He used to talk to Cecilia on the phone and I'd listen while he'd laugh. I'd think he's laughing at me because I'm doing his time."

Though no violence broke between them, Sanders made it known that he was pissed off that Porter had dragged him into his case—and Sanders was watching him.

"I always slept with one eye open," Porter says.

When little Kerry turned eighteen he enlisted in the Marines and was sent to battle in Iraq just as the war was reaching a boiling point. The anxiety was almost too much for Porter. "There were all these body counts. Every time it came on CNN, I'd be like, 'Oh God, please, don't let it be my son.'"

Porter got word that little Kerry once missed a car bomb by a few hundred yards, and that some of his friends died in the blast. "I would watch the funerals on TV with dread, and here I am in penitentiary doing time for a murder I didn't do, and these guys are out there fighting for our lives. And, oh my God, it was just horrible." Porter used to worry about other relatives dying, too, particularly his mother.

"The worst thing that can happen to you is the chaplain comes around and knocks on your door," he says. "Right before I got out, I was in the TV room and I looked up to see someone coming in the front door. It was the chaplain. He kind of looked at me and I got this feeling inside. Then he starts walking my way, so I go rushing to my room. I was in dorm five and he came down the hall looking for a room, and I'm thinking, *Oh my God, please pass me up.*

"And when he finally did pass me up, it was such a relief. Like, man, I'm too close for anything stupid to happen now."

Porter had written to the Kentucky Innocence Project in 2000, and in the fall of 2006 the organization signed him as a client after it became clear that much of the material prosecutors used to convict him was tainted. The lawyers found out the eyewitness Kenneth Brown had picked Porter out of a photo lineup only after being shown a photo of him two days earlier. And Greg Gully's identity as a government informant had never been revealed to Porter's defense lawyer. If it had, she easily could have used that to discredit him.

The wheels began to turn when Kentucky Innocence lawyer Melanie Lowe and others representing Porter met with Louisville Metro Police Sgt. Denny Butler, who had a lot of pull in the DA's office. Butler, who was then looking into a series of murder cases orbiting around Juan Leotis Sanders, agreed to investigate Porter's case. Among his findings was that the duct tape used to make the homemade silencer did not have Porter's DNA on it.

But it wasn't until 2010, when Porter was at Eastern Kentucky Correctional Complex in West Liberty, that a major development effectively smashed Porter's conviction to smithereens.

As part of their investigation, Sgt. Butler and his team had been asking around about a hit man named Ricky Kelly, who worked for a powerful drug operation and allegedly killed eight people in Louisville. In March of that year, the investigators interviewed an associate of Kelly's named Francois Cunningham.

During the interview, Cunningham—who had been a heavy hitter in the crack business in the 1990s—mentioned how in 1996, Juan Leotis Sanders offered him $50,000 to kill Tyrone Camp so that Sanders and his girlfriend Cecilia could cash in on Camp's life insurance. Sanders showed Cunningham how the murder could be carried out using a silencer made out of carpet and duct tape. Cunningham declined to do the job.

A few days later, Sanders told Cunningham that he'd killed Camp, using the very kind of silencer he'd described.

"Kerry Porter did not kill Tyrone Camp," Cunningham told Sgt. Butler.

Butler did not pass this information on to Porter's lawyers right away, despite what it meant for his innocence case. But a *Louisville Courier-Journal* reporter named Andrew Wolfson discovered the statement anyway and banged out a story that ran on August 30, 2011. In it, he quoted Porter's lawyer Melanie Lowe as saying, "It makes me feel sick," that she was hearing about Cunningham for the first time from a reporter. The article said prosecutors had failed in their legal requirement to turn over any evidence that might prove the defendant's innocence.

Sgt. Butler told the *Courier-Journal* that the statement had not been disclosed to Porter because it was part of an "ongoing investigation." A subsequent story quoted the commonwealth's attorney Dave Stengel saying the rules calling for the turning over of such evidence only applied to the period before trial. He said Sgt. Butler held onto the statement because it could endanger Cunningham's life.

The revelation of the Cunningham statement sped things up. "I saw my name in the paper and it looked like I was gonna be acquitted," Porter says. "I just knew in two to three weeks that I was gonna be out. Case workers were calling me into the office like, 'You said this from the very beginning, and everything you said was true.'"

The Jefferson County Commonwealth Attorney's Office announced that they were "moving in the direction of clearing Mr. Porter, but we are not there yet."[3]

On Saturday night, December 3, Porter's family and Camp's family united for a vigil to demand Porter's release. Though Camp's twin brother Jerome had originally suspected Porter as the killer, he'd changed his mind after the indictment and had eventually become one of Porter's biggest supporters, even testifying on his behalf at his trial. "An innocent man is in prison for a crime he didn't commit," Jerome told reporters that night. "Like I said fifteen years ago, I knew who did it, but the prosecuting attorney wouldn't listen to me. It's time for justice to be served."[4]

And Porter's mother Janice said, "It's been almost fifteen years since my son's been incarcerated. And this is a long time—we've both suffered so much. The Camp family needs closure. They can't get closure until we've got justice. My son needs justice."[5]

Two weeks and two days later, Janice got her wish.

It was the Monday before Christmas. Porter's lawyers met with Sgt. Butler and a Kentucky prosecutor in a conference room. Butler said he'd completed his investigation and concluded that Kerry Porter did not kill Tyrone Camp. That same day the attorneys stood before Jefferson County Circuit Judge Irvin Maze and asked that Porter's conviction be vacated and the charges be dismissed. The judge granted the motion. He ordered Porter to be released "immediately and without delay."[6]

When Porter got out of bed that morning, he felt a buzz in the air. "Everybody was acting strange," he says. "I come to work in the law library and my boss was asking me some things he never really asked me. 'Do you know where your cassette tapes are? Where's all your legal work? Make sure nobody else got it.'"

His caseworker then told him he needed to go back to his cell and wait to see a psychologist.

"A psychologist? For what?" Porter asked.

"Just go back to your room," the caseworker said.

Man something's going on here, Porter thought. "And I was feeling from a higher power like it was going to happen, but I didn't want to get my hopes up at the same time because they came crashing down too many times."

Earlier that day, Melanie Lowe had broken the news to Janice by telling her, "I have a Christmas present for you."

"My baby?" Janice had replied.[7]

When Porter got his mother on the phone, her voice sounded electric. But she didn't let on that she was, at that moment, in a car on the way to pick her son up from prison.

"Mama, how you doing?" Porter asked.

"I'm fine, how you doing?"

"I'm doing fine," he said. "Listen, something funny's going on. Can you call around and see what's going on?"

Janice told him to call her back in half an hour. He did, and she said she hadn't been able to get a hold of anybody.

A little while after that, an officer approached Porter's cell.

"Kerry Porter, are you tired of being here?" the officer asked.

"Yeah."

"Then pack your stuff and get out of here."

"What are you doing, shipping me?" Porter asked.

"No," the officer said. "You're going home."

Traditionally, inmates give most of their stuff away when they leave prison. Not Porter.

"I took my cooler, my CD player, a bunch of CDs, all my legal work, legal books, newspaper articles, headphones, TV, typewriter, razors, hygiene stuff," he says. "I think you should keep everything, because that's what reminds you you never want to go back."

He even kept most of his commissary food—ramen noodles, nutty bars, cans of chili, spam, mackerel. And to hell with what the inmates thought about it. "You take those home, you're beyond petty in their eyes, like who's gonna eat prison food at home?" Porter says. "But my position was listen, my people paid for this. Whether I eat it or not I'm gonna take it home and when they do a documentary about my life, that's where it'll be at."

Porter's mother and two friends were waiting for him outside the walls, along with a TV reporter. He embraced his mother tightly. The reporter asked what the first thing was that he'd do as a free man.

"I'm going down to get a Big Mac," he said.

And that's what he did.

"And I ate it slow and embraced the feeling of being free," he says. "You lost so much time, you don't believe it. I ain't in handcuffs, and most of all I do not have a black box on me—that's the thing they lock you down to your waist with a big old Master lock hooked to you and these big heavy dog chains. And I'm looking down and I'm not wearing orange; I'm in this sweat suit they gave me, grey, with a blue Dickey coat. And I've got on my famous hat."

The famous hat was a grey baseball cap with loose strings hanging from the brim. In 2007, a friend who owed Porter money but couldn't pay up gave him the hat instead, and Porter came to consider it a good luck charm. So he never washed it or cut off the loose threads. "It was my signature," he says. "I was known for that. Guys who would come from other penitentiaries would be told, 'He's always gonna have a frayed hat on. That's how you know who Kerry Porter is.'"

It was dark by the time they started the 165-mile drive back to Louisville. Porter took in the night sky and all the lights whizzing by. As they got closer to town, his friend Jackie and her boyfriend Dino pointed out how the landscape had changed, how brick face had become popular with all the new houses that had sprung up.

But Porter was more fascinated by the car he was in. "I'm looking at the new technology of the radio, the touch-button CD player. And keep in mind I used to be a car thief, so I'm looking at all this new anti-theft technology—the steering wheel column that you can't steal no more."

He fooled around with the other passengers' smartphones' touchscreens, while they watched, amused. "I'm like, 'Oh my God, what do you mean you can do this? Why's this screen rolling up and down?' It was a big, stunning thing to see them roll the screens side to side and up and down."

When they finally made it to Porter's sister's house, where she agreed he'd stay until he got back on his feet, he and his mother did more interviews. His mother remarked to reporters, "Every time he called, he would lift me up because he was always positive."[8]

Porter explained why he'd been so positive. "Bitterness will eat you up," he said. "It's cancerous. It's going to eat you up from the inside out."[9]

"You're dealing with so many emotions," Porter says about the day he got out of prison, and the days and weeks that followed. "I'm happy, I'm sad, I'm excited, I'm anxious, I'm—Oh my God—depressed. Somebody's smiling, I'm smiling. Somebody says, 'Damn, you did fifteen years?' I'm back to sad again. Then I hear, 'Hey, Baby, you're home,' and then I'm back to being excited."

The hardest moments came while his sister was off working double shifts as a nurse practitioner. "I was not used to the quietness," he says. "The still just killed me. I was scared to go to sleep because I was scared that when I woke up, this was only gonna be a dream and I would be back in the penitentiary."

On his third night alone in the house, he couldn't sleep so he went downstairs. "I try to turn the TV on, but they got two or three remotes. When I left the street, there was only one remote. I broke down crying that night. I said, 'This is crazy. I can't even turn the TV on.'

"I was ready to commit myself to an institution. It was too much for me. Because your mind wonders so much why this happened to you. Did you do something wrong to contribute to it? You question everything, and that just rings in your head like a .22 bullet bouncing around your brain."

For fifteen years, Porter's life's mission had been simply to win a ticket out of hell. With the mission complete, he faced the scariest question of all: I'm out of penitentiary—what now? "I don't have that drive anymore. I used that energy for so long, I didn't know what I was gonna do without that energy. I'm a fish out of water; I can't swim anymore, and all I did was swim.

"So now, OK, I guess I can go back to laying bricks. But the love was fighting for freedom and there was no other satisfaction greater than that."

Laying bricks didn't look too promising anyway. When he left the street, he was making $13.50 an hour. When he got out all the old brick crews were gone, replaced by cheap labor from Mexico. He finally settled on cutting grass for a living, as he waits on a lawsuit against the city of Louisville and eight police officers for fabricating evidence, using tainted eyewitness testimony, and hiding evidence from his lawyers.

It eats Porter up, not speaking to little Kerry since that day in court so many years ago.

The boy never visited his father in prison—and who could blame him? His mother hated her ex, and little

Kerry's only paternal memories revolved around a lemon of a dad who never came through.

No amount of legal work could undo the damage Porter did as a deadbeat dad. That's what hurts more than anything, even more than going to prison for a crime he didn't commit.

Of the many stories from Porter's life that are hard to tell, this one's the hardest: Little Kerry was eight years old and Christmas was right around the corner. Porter had made some extra cash laying bricks and had promised he was going to buy his son a BB gun.

Then some girl called and Porter went over and did drugs with her, and before you know it he spent all the money. "I had one friend who was going to get me some money but I had too much pride. I thought something would shake."

Nothing shook. On Christmas Day, Porter had nothing to give little Kerry. So he did the only thing he could think of: playing dead on the couch. Little Kerry kept trying to wake his father up, laughing, thinking when Porter opened his eyes he'd reach underneath a couch cushion and pull out a shiny new BB gun.

This went on for way longer than it should have. The boy's cousin, who evidently figured out what was really going on, pulled little Kerry away from his father to distract him with something else. Little Kerry had gotten other toys, but Porter believes all his son really wanted for Christmas was for him to be the father he was supposed to be.

"I never could face him and tell him that I didn't have the BB gun. I just let him see for his own self. That was twenty years ago, but it still emotionally messes with me now. And I reflect on that all the time now.

"I use the downsides, negative thoughts like that, the horriblest time of my life, to keep me strong now. Because

I remember those days, and if those days were that bad it could have been worse."

Chapter 9

VIRGINIA LeFEVER
Ohio, 21 Years

One winter day in 1983, Virginia LeFever gave birth to a girl and named her Rachel. The newborn was good natured, a hearty eater, and a sound sleeper. But after a few weeks, LeFever noticed something unusual about the muscle tone in Rachel's feet—something so subtle she couldn't even place what it was.

When LeFever brought the baby to her pediatrician, the doctor took one look and his eyes darkened. He told her to rush Rachel to the children's hospital. Doctors there confirmed the worst: Rachel had the rare Werdnig Hoffman disease, a genetic deterioration of the spinal cord that usually causes death in infants within months after birth.

The baby's day-to-day decline was shocking and unbearable to watch. In May of that year, LeFever and the four-month-old were given a special room in Licking Memorial Hospital in Newark, Ohio. The mother rocked her daughter until she stopped breathing.

"I had been a nurse since 1980, and in my very early days, I would encounter eighty-year-old women who would still weep when they talked about losing children," says LeFever, her voice starting to crack. "Can you imagine holding that child in your arms while she breathes her last, and you're just helpless to do anything about it?"

If Rachel's death had been the only tragedy in Ginny LeFever's life, it still easily would have made it a terribly sad life. But there were so many other tragedies.

LeFever had a severely disabled son named Jamey who was only nine when, in 1986, he died at home following a seizure caused by bleeding in his brain. And in the years that followed, LeFever lost three more children.

But not to death.

They just vanished, one by one, while their mother served a life sentence for a murder she did not commit. Corey was the first to stop visiting, about a year into his mother's sentence. Sarah followed shortly after. Alex, the youngest, visited for the last time during his mother's fourth year.

LeFever lost her kids because they'd come to believe she had killed their father. She swore she didn't do it, but so many others countered that she did—family friends, neighbors, and of course the judge who sentenced her.

"When the kids stopped coming, it was absolutely the end of the world for me," LeFever says. "It was almost like when Rachel and Jamey had died. It was almost like that kind of loss."

Years later, Alex would reunite with his mother. But the other two, Sarah and Corey, only live in LeFever's memory as the sweet children they once were. Chubby Sarah, who played with Cabbage Patch Kids and sucked her thumb well beyond when it was age-appropriate, bore no resemblance to the woman who said this to a TV reporter after LeFever was freed in 2010: "I honestly believe she deserves to be in prison...she took my childhood from me. She took my father from me."[1] Skinny little Corey, who covered his bedroom walls with dinosaur pictures and slept in a bed shaped like a race car, refused to look at his mother when he gave a deposition for her civil case against the state in 2013. He had not seen her in more than twenty years.

"I left behind an eight-year-old who said I was the best mother in the world," LeFever says of Corey. "Now I've got this sullen adult sitting across from me who thinks I'm the lowest of the low who murdered his dearly departed father."

Corey's deposition took place in the morning, and then Sarah gave hers in the afternoon. LeFever was forbidden from speaking to either to avoid swaying their testimony, so she kept her mouth shut and just stole quick glances. "Seeing them should have been a nice cue-the-violins moment, a nice, tender family reunion, but it was just profoundly sad," she says. "I lost my kids a long long time ago. The children I knew and loved just don't exist anymore."

Well before all of this, LeFever's life was a Sunday night Midwestern tearjerker starring an alcoholic father, an abusive mother, and a brother who shot himself in the head when he was nineteen.

By the time she was twenty-five, she was a divorcée with two kids, one of whom, Jamey, was severely disabled and needed frequent trips to the hospital to treat intracranial hemorrhages. LeFever was unemployed, out of cash and desperate when she met a man named Bill LeFever one night at a club. "He wasn't terribly physically attractive. He had nice eyes, but he was kind of balding and a little chubby. But I didn't care. I just thought he was a nice guy," she says.

She and Bill danced together, had a couple of beers, and he asked her out on a date. Other dates soon followed. "It became this great whirlwind thing and he was going to take care of all my problems," LeFever says. And for a while, she believed he'd pull it off. Bill was an all right guy with a solid factory job manufacturing baby products. And though he was divorced, he remained a doting father to his three kids.

He doted on LeFever's children, too, and that really impressed her. "He just seemed very kind, very caring, really good with the kids—especially Jamey."

Then, one day, Jamey got sick again and had to go to the hospital. LeFever panicked because the health insurance from her old job had run out.

"Well, I've got really good insurance," Bill said. "How about we get married?"

LeFever couldn't think of a reason to say no. Five months after they met, Ginny and Bill tied the knot. She was twenty-six and he was thirty-one.

The early years of marriage were the happiest of her life. She found a new job as a cardiac care nurse. Bill was caring and attentive, helping with the groceries, showing up for dinner on time, and taking her and the kids to his softball games where they'd cheer along with the families of Bill's coworkers.

"He seemed too good to be true," LeFever says.

And he was.

The problems started as they often do, with Bill growing distant and finding excuses not to do any of the housework. But then he started acting paranoid, listening in on his wife's phone conversations and going through her purse. "He was controlling in a lot of different ways and it got to be a pattern of behavior with him," LeFever says.

Had that been the worst of it, the marriage might have worked out. But Bill was also a regular pot smoker, and his habit expanded to pills. Then came January 13, 1983, the day infant Rachel died. Beside himself with grief, Bill learned the same day that his father had died of a heart attack. It was all too much; he stopped showing up to work and swan dived into a drug habit that he'd never emerge from.

"It just went downhill from there. Meanwhile, I'm trying to work and support the family and deal with my own grief and depression," LeFever says.

One night, a minor fight escalated into a major one, and LeFever saw a rabid look in Bill's eyes. She ran into the bedroom and tried to shut the door, but he got there before she was able to. He knocked her down, sat on her chest and put his hands around her throat. LeFever lost consciousness. When she woke up, Bill was gone. Three days later, she asked for a divorce.

The odd events of September 20, 1988, would be disputed at great length during LeFever's murder trial.

Bill came over in the afternoon to collect the last of his belongings. He watched the spooky movie *Lady in White* with the kids and then fell asleep on the sofa. When he woke up, LeFever told him she was taking the kids to bed and he'd better be gone when she came back downstairs. But half an hour later, he was still there. Not in the mood to fight, LeFever left him on the sofa and went to bed.

It was still dark when eight-year-old Corey woke up his mom. "There's something wrong with Dad," he said. LeFever found Bill naked and unconscious on the bathroom floor, having apparently fallen out of the shower. There was water everywhere.

"I was just mad at him because he made such a mess— one more thing I've got to clean up," she says. "It never occurred to me that it was anything other than business as usual for him. I've seen him in worse states over the years."

Bill did not make the cleanup easy as he mumbled nursery rhymes and plucked imaginary objects out of the air—again, nothing LeFever hadn't seen before. She left Bill where he was and went back to bed. At about six o'clock, she went downstairs to make coffee, and noticed her old prescription bottle for the antidepressant amitriptyline on the floor.

When she'd stopped taking the medication a few years earlier, there had been a couple dozen pills left. Now only half a pill remained.

LeFever's drug handbook told her that Bill's stomach had probably already absorbed the amitriptyline, so she called the family physician, who recommended she call an ambulance. LeFever did, and then left to go to work.

The next morning, she got a phone call to come to the hospital because Bill was taking a turn for the worse. Shortly after she arrived, doctors notified her that her soon-to-be ex-husband had died. "The family doctor met me at the doors of the ICU and said, 'I can't believe this.' I said, 'I can't believe it either. It's been over thirty hours since he took the pills. Why now?' And that became the great mystery of the ages."

That mystery spurred a ten-week police investigation, in which LeFever became a prime suspect because she'd been with Bill the night he got sick. Detectives questioned everyone they could find that knew her—neighbors, work-mates, the family doctor.

"I never imagined in a million years that I was going to be charged," LeFever says. "I knew I hadn't done anything to Bill. And eventually they'd rule it as a suicide, the investigation would be over, and I'd move on with the kids."

On December 1, 1988, LeFever was about to join a friend for a de-stressing walk in the woods when she heard a pounding on her door. It was the police announcing she was under arrest for murder.

Everything happened so fast after that. After getting

booked at the police station, LeFever was arraigned and then locked in the Licking County jail to await trial.

She waited four hundred twenty-seven days.

"The whole thing just seemed unreal, like a *Twilight Zone* experience," LeFever says. "Every day was like the day before and nothing shifted." She quickly gave up trying to come to terms with the surreality of what was happening and lost herself in the novels of Sidney Sheldon, Robin Cook, and whatever other authors the jail library had in stock. She read all day in her cell or in the dayroom, wrapped in a blanket, cut off from everything around her.

Meanwhile, reports from the toxicologist were stating that LeFever had poisoned her husband by injecting the antidepressants into his body—a claim she thought was laughable. More troubling was the lack of communication with her kids. Her boss had taken them in, but now LeFever could never seem to get them on the phone.

The courtroom was packed each day of the two-and-a-half-week trial. Spectators included reporters from the *Newark Advocate* and the *Columbus Post Dispatch*. It was the first murder trial in Licking County in four years.

While an overdose of prescription pills might have seemed like the most logical cause of Bill's death, prosecutors described a much more elaborate scenario. They told jurors that after LeFever had injected the antidepressant into Bill's buttocks, she grew impatient when he didn't die right away. So, like Wile E. Coyote, she tried one hairbrained thing after another: she inserted arsenic pellets into his rectum, locked him in a room bombed with pesticide fumigant, and finally went back to the basics and just beat him savagely.

But Bill refused to die. So she gave up and called an ambulance.

This bizarre tale of a bumbling wannabe murderer was largely drawn by the conclusions of toxicologist James L. Ferguson, the prosecution's star witness. Ferguson explained that it was ultimately the antidepressant that killed Bill. He said only an injection of the medication would account for how the drug increased in strength in his system while he was in the hospital.

The defense attorneys argued that LeFever had no motive to kill her husband; the couple was five days from divorce, and she was planning to move to California with the kids. They pointed out Bill's drug addiction, his obvious instability, his depression. They mentioned that Bill had scrawled creepy love messages on LeFever's mirror in a flamboyant bid to win her back. They also presented testimony from a nurse saying she'd heard Bill say he'd ingested the pills and did not want to die.

LeFever wore a black flowered dress the day the verdict came down. Judge Mark Wiest asked her to stand. He said he found her guilty of aggravated murder.

"I felt instantly like my heart had been packed in a container of ice, and there was ice in my veins," LeFever says. "It was the coldest I ever felt in my life."

The judge asked if she would like to say anything before he sentenced her.

"I am shocked at your findings and I continue to maintain my innocence," she said, and passed out cold. A photographer from the *Columbus Post Dispatch* caught the moment in a picture that ran prominently in the next day's edition.

If awaiting trial is like watching a tree sloth load a shotgun, the haul to prison happens as fast as buckshot whizzing out of the barrel. Still in her flowered dress, LeFever was put in a deputy sheriff's car and driven sixty miles west to the Ohio Reformatory for Women in Marysville—the largest

weekends, which meant spending more hours of the day in polyester uniforms that scratched the skin. Another morning, the prison announced that inmates could only wear corrections-issue footwear—a precaution after some male prisoners were caught smuggling drugs in tennis sneakers.

Eventually, inmates had to stop accepting care packages altogether and buy their clothes exclusively from the prison vendor. "They were awful quality products that weren't even second or third tier. They were bottom of the barrel," LeFever says. "Women need bras that fit and shoes that fit. We just need things sometimes. It's the little things in life that give you a little comfort where there isn't any."

No matter how much prison-issue clothing she bought, it wouldn't protect her from the brutal winters. The commissary didn't sell gloves, so LeFever would sleep in her winter jacket with two socks covering each hand. If the flakes were small enough and the wind was right, she would actually get snowed on lying in her bed.

But one adapts.

The inmates had five minutes to shower, so one learned how to quickly get undressed, soap up, shampoo, rinse off, and get her robe back on. If someone went past five minutes, officers came in and dragged her out of the shower. To this day, LeFever gets ready in the morning the same way she did in prison: from taking a shower to blow drying her hair, putting on makeup, and contact lenses—ten minutes. "For women, that's kind of like a world speed record," she says.

Eating was the same way. The inmates would be herded into a giant building called Central Food Service, where they'd line up and have food slapped onto plastic trays. They had fifteen minutes to eat from the moment they sat down. Officers would yell, "Two minutes! You got two minutes! You got to finish your tray! You got to get up now!"

LeFever loved Diet Pepsi, but the rules allowed her just a six-pack every other week. So she worked out a deal with another inmate: two bags of potato chips for a six-pack. "It was an even deal. No one got exploited or used. I wasn't strong arming her and she wasn't bullying me." They kept this up until one day in 1993, when guards got wise to the scheme and locked LeFever in solitary for two and a half weeks. The other woman got more time because it turned out she'd been running an illegal store in her cell.

During the eleven years LeFever spent at the Ohio Reformatory for Women, the rapid rise in crack busts more than doubled the population. The prison was forced to house hundreds of women in massive dorms. LeFever spent one hellish month in one.

"It was like a pole barn with rows and rows and rows of beds," she says. "I could lie on my back and stretch my arm over and touch the bed beside me—that's how close we were. They turned the lights out at ten or eleven and it was supposed to be quiet, but there would be one guard for all of those women and there wasn't any quiet to be had. Just people laughing and carrying on, sometimes having arguments. Mostly they were just loud."

Staying clean wasn't easy when only four showers worked for five hundred women. The worst was waiting in line while inmates used the shower for some quick sex. They'd assign a lookout who'd holler when an officer was coming.

Each inmate got a 2.4-cubic-foot locker box, and you really had to lock up *everything*. Once, LeFever washed a pair of underwear in the sink and hung them up to dry on her bunk. Someone snatched them away when she wasn't looking.

When LeFever went away to Marysville, she was in a crisis over what to do with her kids. Her oldest daughter Heather, who was in college at Ohio State, had offered to take care of the younger ones. But LeFever refused to put the burden on her.

The only other option was putting them with a foster family, so that's what she did—a decision she deeply regretted after becoming convinced the foster parents had brainwashed the kids into thinking their mother was a killer.

When Corey, Sarah, and Alex dropped out of her life, LeFever didn't know what to do with the pain. Then she discovered the therapeutic merits of eating. "It wasn't like food tasted good to me. I was just trying to fill this big hole in my heart. Whatever was in my tray I'd put in my mouth, and then anything anyone around me wasn't going to eat, I'd eat too."

In a year, LeFever went from 190 to 273 pounds. "I was like a beach ball with legs."

After a long time LeFever accepted that the kids were gone for good. So when Corey called her one day in 1999, she says, "You could have knocked me over with a feather. I just couldn't believe he actually called me like that." Corey brought his mother up to date on his life. He'd met a girl named Shawna that he liked so much he quit his job in Ohio and hopped on a Greyhound bus to San Diego to be with her.

After that phone call, LeFever and her son spoke regularly. Then three months in, without giving a reason, Corey stopped accepting her collect calls.

LeFever continued sending emails and birthday cards, and never got a response. Then, one day in May 2006, she got a formally-written email from Corey, who was now a father.

If you and the three of us are to maintain a relationship of sorts you must understand that we still believe and hold you to be guilty. That said, we don't wish harm or burden upon you, he wrote.

If anything, we do wish that you'd be able to enjoy life as a free woman. Regardless of our lot in life, you're our mother and we, your children, sincerely do hope that someday we can share a margarita over some Mexican food and catch up on what we've missed.

The email left LeFever feeling oddly calm. "You know, it really wasn't that surprising," she says. "He never said, 'I've come to my senses,' or whatever. And all the kids heard growing up is that I was guilty."

She wrote back that she loved him, missed him, and hoped one day he would believe that she didn't kill his father.

A week after September 11, 2001, LeFever was up for parole. She was transferred to Franklin Pre-Release Center in Columbus. The parole board heard her out, denied her release, and said come back in ten years. The one ray of light out of that was the warden let her stay at Franklin for the remainder of her sentence. It was a much nicer facility of only five hundred women.

Eight years passed.

On November 21, 2009, LeFever watched an Ohio State Buckeyes game on TV that inadvertently set the course for her freedom. LeFever was always a rabid Ohio State fan —today, her iPhone's ringtone is the Buckeyes' fight song "Across the Field"—and she never missed the team's annual head-to-head against the hated Michigan Wolverines. Ohio State whipped Michigan twenty-one to ten that day. The broadcaster played a prerecorded voiceover from a woman named Stephanie Spielman, who urged viewers to contact the Ohio State Alumni Association about donating to the breast cancer research foundation started by her and husband Chris Spielman, a former Buckeyes star. Stephanie had died of breast cancer the day before the game.

Ohio State Alumni Association. The phrase had jumped out at LeFever.

Alumni. Alumni. Alumni. The word flashed in her mind like a neon Broadway banner. She called her lawyer Kort Gatterdam and they brainstormed something that they hadn't explored before: investigating Ohio State alum James Ferguson, the toxicologist whose wacky murder theory had been key to LeFever's conviction.

It had always troubled LeFever how quickly the judge bought into Ferguson's theory that she had ground up the pills, mixed them with liquid, and injected them into her husband—an arduous process that she found preposterous. In fact, she and her legal team were in the midst of a civil suit challenging those findings.

What if Ferguson was just a quack?

Gatterdam contacted the university's alumni association, and it didn't take long for him to hit the jackpot. Ferguson turned about to be a serial liar, who'd claimed in hundreds of trials that he'd received a biochemistry degree from Ohio State in 1972, when he really hadn't gotten it until 1988—about six months before Bill died. His lousy grades hadn't kept him from lying to employers about his level of education.

Authorities investigated Ferguson and eventually arrested him. He did thirty days in jail—a wrist slap, but his reputation was destroyed. In October of that year, LeFever sued Ferguson, Licking County Coroner Robert Baker, a number of police officers, and local counties for false evidence and depriving her of constitutional rights, including her right to a fair trial.

LeFever's lawyer obtained signed affidavits from a coroner and two toxicologists stating that Ferguson's theory was not scientifically accepted.

A year and a day after the Wolverines-Buckeyes game, Judge Mark Wiest, who had convicted and sentenced LeFever twenty-one years earlier, overturned her conviction and set her free. He wrote in his judgment entry, "This is about fairness. Is it fair to let a verdict stand, when it is based in large part on the testimony of a proven liar?[2] Ferguson was the linchpin holding the state's case together. Without his testimony, the state's case would have fallen apart."[3]

LeFever got out of bed on November 22, 2010, and knew in her heart that this was her last day in prison. She started giving stuff away—her CD player, some CDs, some artwork she'd made. At ten in the morning, the judge faxed the warden an order for LeFever's release.

The warden led LeFever to a corner and quietly told her the news. Breaking protocol, LeFever impulsively put her arms around the smartly-dressed woman and squeezed her tightly.

"You're going to get me in trouble!" the warden shouted.

"I don't care!" LeFever said.

A few more orders of business—returning the prison-issue sheets and uniforms, signing a few forms—and she was done. Because she was so well-known at Franklin, three hundred inmates gathered to see her out. "People were lining up and crying and hugging me. It was really amazing."

Carrying her TV, LeFever walked out the gate with her lawyers into a swarm of cameras. They went straight to the Italian chain restaurant Brio to celebrate. Recollecting what it was like to eat real food again, LeFever can only say, "Oh my God."

"It took my digestive system a few days to adjust," she adds. "It took some time to get used to 'earth food' after all those years of junk."

A friend in Newark took LeFever in, giving her a chance to enjoy the simple pleasures people take for granted. "I couldn't sleep for the first three nights because the bed was too comfortable," she says. Waking up her first morning as a free woman, all she could think about was her dream meal, a western omelet from the breakfast chain Bob Evans. So she ate just that, and afterward made her first dental appointment, and bought her first iPhone. Not long after, she bought a Jeep and a MacBook Pro. Then she moved into her own apartment, a two-bedroom in a building right off the Ohio State campus in Columbus.

"For a little while, I had a hard time adjusting. I felt like I was wearing a costume, where my clothes didn't really belong to me," she says. "But that passed after a couple of weeks."

In June 2011, Licking County Prosecutor Ken Oswalt had LeFever's case dismissed, saying there was not enough evidence "untainted" by Ferguson to retry her. [4]

LeFever, who's back to work as a nurse part time, puts little brainpower in trying to rationalize what happened to her. "I knew that moving on was underway when prison wasn't the first thing on my mind in the morning and the last thing at night," she says. "There are days or even weeks that I don't think about being incarcerated, just like high school doesn't enter my mind every day, or my grandmother. It just doesn't."

Nor do thoughts about James Ferguson, the man whose testimony put her in prison. "I don't know why, but I really don't hate him. I just think he's a sad, pathetic little man. There's too much living to do to be mad. I don't want to invest energy in him anymore."

More important is staying close to her two kids who still speak to her, Heather and Alex, the latter of whom, she says, "has a little bit less of a jaundiced eye just looking at the facts objectively. He's said of Corey and Sarah, 'I don't know why they keep doing this. If they just look, they'll realize they've been manipulated by the people around them.'"

LeFever's wildest hope is that the two middle children will return to her one day, like Alex. But she's not praying for miracles. "I don't think about them every day, and it's sad that I don't. But I've lived with this a long time and I can only tolerate so much pain. I've got to compartmentalize and move on."

But sometimes compartmentalizing is impossible, like on that dark day in 2013, when LeFever's lawyer deposed Corey and Sarah for her civil case. "I knew that they were going to be there and they knew I was going to be there and I just tried to be neutral. I didn't want to say or do anything that could be used against me or hurt their feelings or make them angry," LeFever says.

"Corey wouldn't even give his home address while I was in the room. My thoughts were just like, *Seriously? You think I'm going to hop on a plane to San Diego and stalk you outside your house?*"

In between Corey and Sarah's sessions, LeFever and her lawyer left the courthouse to have lunch. That was the only time of the day LeFever could let her guard down. "I was crying on the way to the restaurant, was crying in the restaurant and was crying on the way back," she says. "Then I put my game face on and went back in there."

Chapter 10

DEVON AYERS
New York, 17 Years

Devon Ayers has a lot of sad stories to tell from all those years he sat behind bars.

He was, in no particular order, stabbed, humiliated, and thrown into solitary confinement for months at a time. And each morning he woke to the horrific reminder that he was serving fifty years for a murder he didn't commit.

But his worst moment in prison? None of the above.

"It would have to be the day my grandma died," the Bronx native says.

Ayers can laugh about all that other stuff now because of the joy—*the joy!*—of knowing it's all in the past. But he can't laugh about his grandma. When he talks about her, his eyes go dark and he's back in Shawangunk Correctional Facility the day his counselor gave him the bad news and everything felt like it was falling apart.

The thing was, when Mattie Ayers died on June 4, 2012, life was starting to look very sunny for her grandson. The double homicide case against him was unraveling quickly. He was about to become a star client of the Manhattan-based Exoneration Initiative, which would spring him from the big house in less than a year.

No matter.

"The day they sentenced me that was like a celebration in comparison to me losing my grandma," he says. "I couldn't imagine life living without her, especially in prison. She used to come see me in the rain, sleet, snow. I said, 'Grandma, you don't need to worry about it.' She said, 'I'm coming.'

"If I was in the mob, she was the boss and I was the capo. There was no person on this earth who was higher."

Ayers is animated and hilarious. He tells prison stories with his whole body, all bulging eyes and flailing arms. During the dark years in prison, Ayers was the guy who'd make you laugh so hard you'd forget all about killing yourself. He was so upbeat all the time, inmates and corrections officers sometimes thought he'd just been handed his "Get Out of Jail" card. "Nope," he'd say—pausing half a second for effect—"I've got a few decades to go."

"I lived by a rule. Let nobody see you sweat, because if you let a person see you sweat, they've got an upper hand over you," he says. "That was my coping mechanism. I learned to be that way.

"When my grandma died, I broke my number one rule; I let them see me sweat. I let them see me cry."

When Devon "Skloop" Ayers was seventeen, he was living in a Bronx neighborhood called Soundview, best known for its large population of gangbangers and drug dealers. He fell naturally into an occupation common among high school dropouts: selling crack on street corners. "I was a typical hustler," he says. "That was my job. That was the only thing I knew I was good at."

But something changed in Ayers when he became a teenage father of a beautiful girl named Barbara. He quit the crack business and lived off his earnings while searching for legit work. All he wanted at that time was be a good parent, a responsible parent.

He's confident now that, prison or no prison, he'd have stayed on the straight path for the rest of his life. But just as Ayers was turning his life around, two people were murdered in his neighborhood, and that changed everything.

On January 18, 1995, police went to the apartment of a Federal Express recruiter named Denise Raymond after her family called concerned that she wasn't showing up to work. They came upon a gruesome sight: Raymond, lying flat on the floor, her wrists handcuffed, her mouth stuffed with a sock and taped over, and two bullet holes in her head.

Two days later, a Senegalese livery car driver named Baithe Diop picked up a fare at West 141st Street in Harlem and drove to the Bronx. When he reached Soundview, the passengers pulled out guns and shot him dead. Diop's 1988 Lincoln kept rolling after the gunmen fled, eventually slamming into a dumpster.

Baithe Diop died about a block from Denise Raymond's home. The subsequent police investigation would link the two murders and herd together a dizzying array of defendants and witnesses. When the investigation was all done, *New York* magazine would laud the fine work of the New York City Police Department with an article entitled, "How to Solve a Murder."

Detectives found two key witnesses. One, a sixteen-year-old girl named Catherine Gomez, said she'd eavesdropped on Ayers and three other guys not only planning Denise Raymond's murder, but boasting about it after. The other witness, a drug-addict named Miriam Tavares, told police she saw Ayers, his three buddies, and two other people fleeing Baithe Diop's car after killing him.

Police would conclude the Denise Raymond murder was a hit job orchestrated by a jealous boyfriend, while the motive for the Diop murder was to throw investigators off the scent of a different crime—the theft of $50,000 of cocaine.

Ayers's three friends Michael Cosme, Carlos Perez, and Israel Vasquez, were picked up, charged and arraigned for murder. Two months later, Ayers's grandmother phoned her grandson and told him, "You'd better run out and pick up a newspaper." Ayers grabbed the first paper he saw, which featured his picture accompanied by these words:

SUSPECT: Devon (Skloop) Ayers Description: Male, 18, 5-feet-6, 130 pounds.1

His knees buckled. *I know I'm doing dirt but I ain't doing murders,* he thought. *I didn't shoot nobody. I'm making money like the average kid in the streets of New York.* Ayers turned himself in at the Forty-Third Police Precinct in the Bronx. News crews got the word and waited outside the building to get shots of police walking the perp out the door to a squad car that would take him to court.

"The police were so anxious to get themselves on camera before bringing me to jail that when we were walking out we had to wait for the camera crew to set up. I tried to keep my head down; I had long braids at the time and police were grabbing a handful of my hair to hold my head up."

Ayers and his codefendants were taken to New York City's massive jail on Rikers Island, where they awaited trial. The wait took two and a half years—typical in an era when New York City crime was so rampant that the courts couldn't keep up with the perp count. "Going over the bridge to Rikers Island was nerve-racking for me," Ayers says. "You get ready to go like Jonah into the whale—but at least Jonah was caught by surprise. You're going in there willingly."

Ayers realized quickly that to survive he had to take his mind off everything but day-to-day matters of jail life. "The first step is jail. The case and the crime, all that stuff don't matter. I'll deal with that later," he says. "Let me deal with making myself a person in jail, so I can be in the right mind frame to fight the case I'm dealing with… because otherwise I'm gonna succumb to the pressures of, *I can't take it anymore*, the pressures of, *If I'm not gonna kill myself, I'm gonna make somebody else kill me*."

He lay awake at night, struggling to fight off those pressures. "Forget the fact that I didn't do the crime I'm in prison for. I just had a kid! I'm family oriented. I can't see my grandma when I want; I can't see my moms when I want; I can't see my kid when I want. I was trying to make a life with a special young lady and it was all taken away."

Just like on the street, Ayers was a hustler at Rikers. But instead of drugs he was hustling commissary—cigarettes, sandwiches, cereal, and other goodies that he peddled at twice their value. It energized him. "I'd say, 'You're looking for some cigarettes right now? I've got three packs in my cell; I'll give you one, but you've got to give me two back at the store.' Or I might say, 'I'll give you one cigarette but you gotta give me five when you go to the store.' Alright, cool."

Or, he says, "I'll buy three dollars' worth of turkey, get some cheese, get some buns, get a couple of sodas—at that time they had the two-liter sodas—and a couple pies. I'll make two sandwiches, a cup of soda and a pie—give me ten dollars for that. *I* didn't pay ten dollars for that. I'm a hustler now."

In May, 1997, Ayers and his three codefendants were put on trial for the murders of Denise Raymond and Baithe Diop. Prosecutors and witnesses painted a convincing portrait of the four men as dangerous street thugs bred to commit cold-blooded murder. The jury ate it up and brought double-murder convictions on all except Vasquez, who was only found guilty for killing Raymond. A subsequent trial would find two additional defendants guilty in the Diop slaying: Ayers's cousin Eric Glisson and a woman named Kathy Watkins.

"They said, 'How do you find the defendant?' and they said, 'Guilty.' You're telling me I'm guilty. I'm guilty on two counts of homicide," Ayers says. "My whole life flashed before me. I'm wondering, how did I get to this stage in my life? That's the first question you ask after you snap back to reality. How did I get here? How did this happen?"

Ayers, Cosme, and Perez were sentenced to fifty years to life and Vasquez to twenty-five to life. Glisson and Watkins would later each be sentenced to twenty-five to life. Ayers was ordered to be shipped sixty miles north to Downstate Correctional Facility in Fishkill, the first of five prisons he'd do time in.

Ayers says, "I really didn't want to go up north because it was unknown to me. I got used to Rikers Island—I wouldn't say it was comfortable, but it had become an environment I'd adapted to. But now I had to leave and go to an environment that's twenty times worse."

Jailhouse buddies who'd been through the prison system on prior convictions gave him a proper Rikers sendoff, scaring his socks off with horror stories about what he'd encounter when he got to Downstate. "Yo, you know they've got dudes up there that'll knock you out and stick it in your booty hole? Dudes that'll knock you out and give you oral sex?" they told Ayers. "You ain't gonna beat this one motherfucker. He's six foot eight and can lift three hundred pounds."

Ayers had had a growth spurt in prison, but he was no offensive lineman. "Man, I ain't but five foot seven and weigh about one hundred fifty-five pounds," he says, laughing about it now. "And he's lifting three hundred? We're gonna have to think about this one."

"I grew up in prison," Ayers says, and then lists off the five New York State lockups he passed through: Downstate, Green Haven, Great Meadow, Attica, Shawangunk.

"Everything you learned before prison, erased. Two percent of what you learned before might help you now. What you learn once you're in is what's gonna get you out alive." Ayers, who'd been a shy and introverted kid on the streets, now saw the value in fraternizing, particularly with the old-timers. "People saw so much potential in me and they knew I was a good individual. They sat me down and were like, 'Yo, I'm gonna invite you into my circle.' I kept company with some real solid people.

"I learned to get a sense of humor, too. Before I got to jail I was really antisocial. But in prison, I became the person who, if you ever need somebody to talk to, you're always gonna make your way around to me. I could look at someone and be like, 'Yo, you ain't yourself today. What's going on?'"

Ayers two best friends in prison were both guys from Brooklyn: Lavonne Smith, convicted of a bike shop robbery in 1994 that resulted in the killing of a police officer (Smith's brother Vernon was found guilty of the murder), and Terrence Rice, convicted of attempted murder after a shootout with cops. "They were the only two dudes I trusted," says Ayers, who maintains that both men are innocent.

Just as friendship was critical to survival, so was making sure a day didn't slip by that Ayers didn't advance himself in some way. Time was too precious to waste, steel bars or no steel bars. "I left the card games and the dice games and domino games alone and I became a peer counselor; I got into the Scared Straight program. I got into transitional services. I found a sense of direction, became Muslim. I even got some college, and if I couldn't pay for it, I still got the college courses, just didn't pay for the tests," he says.

He also worked on his legal case, learned Arabic and sign language, and read every book he could get his hands on. One book that particularly touched him was the Holocaust story *Schindler's List*. "I really read that book. People were like, 'You read that?' Yes, I read it." *Schindler's List* gave him a profound sense of the value of a human life. "These were Jews; these were people. They didn't do nothing wrong, but just because one motherfucker said this is how it should be you're gonna slaughter all these people? Come on, these people are human beings."

Much of his reading was done in solitary confinement, where he estimates he spent between three and four years total for getting into scuffles with rival inmates. His longest stretch in solitary was eight and a half months following a fight.

In solitary, you were cordoned off in a special area of the prison and locked up for twenty-three hours a day. Depending on the facility, you weren't necessarily out of view of other inmates. "It's funny, I can sit back and laugh at it," Ayers says. "There was a dude, he was in the first cell and he would get up early in the morning. He would go all the way to my cell and yell, 'Get up! Yo, wussup? SUCK MY DICK!' I fell for this shit every morning. Every day it became a ritual, just to piss me off early in the morning."

As if reliving the moment, Ayers suddenly blurts out, "I'm gonna kill you!" to the tormenter in his memory. Then he laughs.

"In the box you're like a vampire," he continues. "You sleep all day and you're up all night. We call cell bars the Gate. You're in the Gate talking to someone six cells down from you. In between those six cells you have fifteen different conversations going on, but you manage to hear the conversation with someone six cells down from you."

From 1997 to 1998, when Ayers was at the Green Haven Correctional Facility in Stormville, the typical salary for remedial work like cooking and mopping was fifteen dollars a week. But there was one job that paid a whopping one hundred fifty a week: the cell-building program, a state-wide initiative in which prisons expanded on the cheap by hiring their own inmates as laborers.

When Ayers first arrived at the prison and learned about the cell-building program, he sensed a deal that was too good to be true. So he consulted with the old-timers. "They really sat me down and told me the reality. They were like, 'Yo, man, think about it. You might be building *yourself* a cell. Worse yet, you might be building someone in your family a cell.'"

Violent types who didn't find humor in that irony made sure the young fools who signed up to build the cells knew it. "They'd stab these kids. They'd cut these kids up," Ayers says. But there'd always be newbies to replace those who went to the hospital—or to the grave—thanks to the heartless recruiting tactics of guidance counselors. "These young kids are coming in here and they ain't got shit. They ain't got no family. They ain't got no girl. They ain't got nothing. They go to bed at night and all they got is a goddamn Oodles of Noodles soup in their locker. They want to smoke cigarettes or drink coffee but they ain't got enough for that. All they got is the walls that's looking to devour them. Their counselors would tell them, 'You're supposed to talk to me if you got any problems,' but in the same breath, 'Well, listen, if you want to make some money, I can put you in the cell-building program.'

"They are no different from pimps in the street."

Ayers did a great job keeping himself from getting stabbed until one summer night in 2002 at Great Meadow Correctional Facility in Comstock. He'd just finished dinner and was heading back to his cell when a crew of Latin gangsters surrounded him and stabbed him in eight places on his body.

The crew belonged to the Mara Deas, and their rivalry with a much, much bigger gang, the Bloods, was about to become a lopsided all-out war. The Mara Deas needed to get out of Great Meadow quickly, and there was one surefire way to make that happen. "It wasn't like something that me and them initiated, or that we had some beef prior to that. They just came at me as an easy way to get out of the prison," Ayers says.

"I was in my comfortable state. Everybody knows you shouldn't be comfortable in prison…as we were walking to the cell block I see one of the Spanish dudes handing out knives to his people. I didn't pay it no mind because it had nothing to do with me. In my mind you ain't that stupid to come at me like that. I was big headed."

The knives were as sharp as ice picks. They could have been made from anything—twisted-together spokes from a fan grate or rods of metal pried out from between floor ties, the ends ground to a deadly-sharp point.

An old-timer saw the men eyeballing Ayers and warned him to watch his back. "They're acting up," he said. "We can be together to make sure nothing happens to you."

"I don't care about the dudes," Ayers said. "That shit ain't got nothing to do with me."

What happened next took only seconds, but Ayers remembers it in slow motion. As he made a turn to go up the next flight of stairs, one of the men grabbed him and put him in a headlock. As Ayers struggled, he saw another guy coming his way with a knife. "When put in a situation like that I have to think of all my vital parts," Ayers says. "I'm like, cool, he's got his hand around my neck so he can't stab me in the neck. That's one vital part. My face I can block."

The thug stabbed Ayers on the right side of his abdomen. *Oh shit, that really hurt!* was his first thought, followed by, *Let me get this motherfucker off me so I can deal with this dude with the knife.*

"So I get the motherfucker off me—the dude that had me in a headlock," he says, "and I'm going after the dude with the knife. Me and him start squaring off and I'm trying to get the knife, but I'm paying attention to what's going around me as well."

Other Mara Deas were circling, so Ayers broke away and ran for it. "I ain't no super tough motherfucker and I damned sure ain't no Man of Steel, so I ran around the corner and called a friend. As I'm going around the corner there was a dude on the phone."

It didn't occur to Ayers that nobody ever used the phone during chow time because the phones weren't running then. The dude clobbered him on the head with the receiver. Ayers went down and five Mara Deas descended and tore into him like hyenas. "Yo, dudes, what's this all about?" Ayers screamed.

"Then I felt like they were punching me," he says, "but in all reality they were stabbing the shit out of me. The stab wounds felt like punches. They were all over my arms, my right side; one dude stabbed me in my buttocks."

Corrections officers came running and the scrum eased off. But just then one more gangster charged at Ayers. "I tried to throw one or two punches but I had lost a lot of blood at that time. I hit him but it wasn't hard enough to knock him out. It was hard enough to shock him. And that's when everything went black." Ayers was hospitalized with stab wounds on his rib cage, hip, elbow, and arm.

But he came out of it OK. The gangsters, not as well, he says. "It worked out worse for them. They didn't realize how far my hands could reach. I had friends in every jail. There were a lot of people who had a lot of love for me."

After the stabbing, Ayers was transferred to Shawangunk, where he'd stay from 2004 until his release in 2013.

During a stint in solitary one day, he was reading a transcript from his trial when he hit upon a hard realization. "At the end of my reading, I found myself guilty," he says.

"Deep inside, you know you had nothing to do with this case. But from an unbiased opinion, my own opinion, damn, did I just convict myself? Yes, I did. I found the defendant guilty. And I had to process why I found myself guilty."

In their determination to win a conviction, the prosecutors had put on a masterful performance framing Ayers and his codefendants as bloodthirsty hell-raisers terrorizing the streets of the Bronx. "The impression they leave you with was this is a solid gang, and what they do is instill fear in the community. They steal. They kill. So you have an innocent little girl on the stand who doesn't speak too much English, and she's telling you we're part of a ruthless gang that ran the neighborhood, and she's still afraid. She can't look at us face to face. How much of the evidence are you really gonna listen to?

"The prosecution took my mind completely off the evidence and had me focus on fear, fear, fear. Not, were they at the scene of the crime? Not, did they find a gun? They totally lost that. They didn't convict me on evidence. They convicted me on the look on the witness's face. *She's scared. Do you want to be scared?*"

"What can you do?" he says when asked how it felt to convict himself. "If you're on a deserted island, outside of fighting to get off by swimming or building a raft, what else are you gonna do—kill yourself? Or are you gonna live with it? You're gonna find some way to adjust and adapt to that island, no matter how big it is. You're gonna find a way because your instinct is you want to live."

The events that led to the exoneration of Ayers and his codefendants started in 2003, when a Bronx cop-turned federal-investigator named John O'Malley was investigating a gang called Sex Money and Murder. Two cooperating members, Jose Rodriguez and Gilbert Vega, told O'Malley that they had robbed and shot a livery car driver in late 1994 or early 1995. They did not know the driver's name or whether he died. O'Malley had little to go on.

Nine years passed.

In May 2012, Ayers's cousin Eric Glisson, who was serving twenty-five years for his supposed role in Diop's murder, wrote a letter to federal investigators saying he'd heard Diop's killers were members of Sex Money and Murder. The letter got passed to O'Malley, who immediately made the connection to what Rodriguez and Vega had told him years earlier.

The next month, the Bronx DA's office reopened the murder investigation. Much had come to the surface since 1997. The sixteen-year-old witness Catherine Gomez had recanted her testimony, admitting she'd given it under duress. The other witness, Miriam Tavares, had since died. Call records from Diop's cell phone revealed that after he was killed, the phone was used to call associates of Rodriguez and Vega.

These facts were enough to spring Eric Glisson and Kathy Watkins from prison on bond in October 2012.

In December, charges against Glisson, Watkins, Ayers, Cosme, and Perez were dropped in Diop's murder.

Meanwhile, lawyers from the Exoneration Initiative were looking into the murder of the other victim, Denise Raymond. They read testimony in old trial transcripts from the victim's friend Kim Alexander, who said that she, Raymond, and Raymond's jealous ex-boyfriend all rode down the elevator in her building together the night she died.

Prosecutors had used this testimony to suggest that the ex-boyfriend, Charles McKinnon, then alerted Ayers and his buddies that Raymond was leaving so they'd be able to ambush her when she got home.

In his own trial, McKinnon was acquitted largely because a security video from that night contradicted Alexander's testimony; it showed only her and Raymond—but not McKinnon—exiting the building. That video never resurfaced after he walked free.

When the Bronx District Attorney reopened the investigation years later, the New York City Police Department turned over the security video, which had until then never been shown to the lawyers for Ayers, Cosme, and Perez. The Exoneration Initiative lawyers filed a motion to drop the convictions, arguing that the security video should have been handed over years earlier. They also argued that because authorities had linked the two murders—incorrectly, as it turned out—the jury might have been unduly influenced by one to convict on both.

The District Attorney agreed that the convictions should be vacated. On January 23, 2013, Ayers and his codefendants were bussed to Bronx Supreme Court—none knowing that this was a one-way trip. "No one told us we were going home that day," Ayers says. "They told us we were going to be home by maybe February."

So it was surprising to see members of his and the other defendants' families packing the courtroom. Ayers's half brother, who'd never missed a court date, was crying. Exoneration Initiative director Glenn Garber could barely contain himself as he whispered, "Did you hear?"

"What are you talking about?" Ayers asked.

"You're going home today," Garber said.

Ayers was too stunned for tears. He turned to Cosme and said, "Oh God, this can't be happening. It's happening for real."

Ayers has difficulty describing how it felt to hear the judge grant him his freedom. "Every word the judge said, I couldn't process. I felt so alive. Not to say I felt dead before, but I felt *alive*," he says.

Then, as these things often go, one last bureaucratic regulation killed the buzz. The defendants were told they had to be bussed back to prison before the release was final. On the cusp of freedom, the two men went berserk. "Me and Mike were like, 'We were released today from this courthouse. We want to be released!'" Ayers says.

Cosme told the corrections officers, "If we have to go upstate I'm gonna die in this cell tonight. The judge told us we were going home. He didn't say, 'Go back up north and go home.' He said, 'You're leaving here *today*.'"

A sympathetic officer who'd known the defendants all the way back from their conviction seventeen years earlier decided to take a stand. He called their lawyers, who got busy making calls of their own. It took several hours, but the judge finally ordered that the men be released then and there. The friendly veteran corrections officer insisted he have the honor of walking them out of prison. But first, they changed out of their prison clothes into sharp Nike outfits their families had bought for them.

"The first person who ran under that gate, ran through

everybody, was my little girl," Ayers says. "It felt so real to hold her as a free man as opposed to giving her hugs in the visiting area."

"You dreamt of the day and when it finally comes, the feeling is unexplainable. You can't say how you felt. It's impossible to say how you felt."

Ayers went back to his grandma's apartment that night and clung to eighteen-year-old Barbara as if she was still a newborn. "She fell asleep and I watched her all night."

"You know what the first thing that I really enjoyed doing when I came home was?" Ayers asks. "Are you ready for this?

"Taking out the garbage.

"In jail you don't take out the garbage. To walk the garbage to the incinerator or walk the garbage outside, it was amazing. When you were a kid and your mother used to tell you take out the garbage, you'd be like 'Oh, come on, Mom, I don't want to go outside. I don't have time!'"

Ayers is still astounded by all the changes in the world. "Metro cards, cell phones, the list goes on. I look at how people dress, how they interact with each other. I see how the world has changed since I left. Everything is new to me."

All told, he feels like he adjusted back into society pretty quickly for a guy who was cut off from civilization for seventeen years. "I run into people who say, 'I can't believe you spent that much time in prison,'" Ayers says. "Well, I'm good at adapting. No, I'm not gonna say I'm good at adapting. I'm gonna say I'm blessed."

Blessed with a sense of humor and a sunny outlook, and landing a job out of prison that he absolutely loves: taking care of mentally challenged people for a mental health and social services agency. He's also blessed with a special woman, his fiancée Aisha, who stuck with him through everything.

And Ayers feels ever-so-blessed that he gets to tell one particular story about freedom, one that only a truly free man could tell. A year after getting released from prison, Ayers, his mother, Aisha, and her daughter flew to Africa to visit Aisha's family.

The pleasure of being there—in Sierra Leone, a place unlike any Ayers had ever been—was one of the very greatest he'd ever felt. Some people travel to far-off places hoping that they can replicate the feeling of wonder they felt every day as kids. For a man serving a fifty-year sentence, that's a pleasure so unattainable that he doesn't dare dream of it.

"Every day was a new adventure for me," Ayers says. "Waking up every morning, looking out the window and seeing that view. I was so intrigued by what I seen. We had transportation and all that stuff but I was walking out there with the people, laughing and joking with them like I knew these people for years.

"I seen a lizard and a cat have a fight over some grains of rice. I watched that for an hour and a half and can't tell you who won the fight. I sat on the porch and watched people trying to give their kids to me, trying to give themselves to me. At end of the day, I'm going in my pockets saying, 'Let me buy you a pair of slippers.'

"Or, we're cooking some American food, I see some kids who don't eat American food. I give them some spaghetti and meatballs, and they loved that. It wasn't like they were homeless, like they didn't have food in their stomachs. But we shared food.

"The day before we left," he says, "I went off in the darkness. I didn't know where I was going; I just wanted to get lost so I could have an excuse for why I didn't have to leave."

"Am I upset? I'm very upset. I did a lot of time in prison for a crime I didn't commit. But look what came out of it. I got a beautiful woman. I got kids that drive me out of my mind. I'm completely educated. I came from a different style of life and look at me now. Prison changed me into the better person."

"I just got rid of my pride," he says when asked how. "If a man tells you, 'Bend over, let me look in your ass,' are you really gonna have pride after that? This is a man who was just telling you, 'I'll kill you, you aren't worth shit.' You're really gonna have pride after that? Pride gets your ass killed, in and out of prison. You're way better off without it.

"Pharaoh had so much pride, he went and followed the nigger into the middle of the ocean. Do you see boats out there? If Moses did that and you can't do that, why are you going out into that water?"

Ayers's grandmother Mattie, who died in her late nineties, was one of the few who believed him all along when he said, "I didn't do it." He wishes more than anything that she could have lived to see him unshackled.

He doesn't speak as fondly of other relatives, like his aunts, who he says only pretended they believed him. "Behind my back they were always like, 'That's what you get when you hang out with the wrong people.' They didn't believe me, but they'd lie to my face and mock my intelligence, which I really hate.

"But guess what? At the end of the day, we're still family. But I'm gonna keep you at arm's length.

"My grandma and my moms, they were like my number-one supporters. I would never lie to them about anything. If they said I was selling drugs, I'd be like, 'Yeah I am, Grandma, I'm selling drugs.' See, I confess to that because these are people who have my best interests in mind and I know they love me. Without them I'm alone in this world.

"To this day, I still feel alone in this world without my grandma. I haven't been to her gravesite because I'm not strong enough to do it."

Grandma taught Ayers how to cook and to knit. Grandma, who grew up in Jim Crow Georgia, taught him not to hate. She taught him how important education was. "She showed me that, listen, you have to make decisions for yourself. Nobody can live your life but you. So the decisions that you make in life—that shit don't reflect on anybody else; that shit reflects on you."

Above all, Grandma taught him the importance of family.

"It took me up until the day she died for me to realize she was telling me to hold this family together no matter what," Ayers says. "They could be drug addicts, idiots, nincompoops, self-righteous, conceited, but at end of the day they're family, and if you ain't got family, you ain't got shit in this world. Family lets you know you're a part of something."

CONCLUSION

Something needs to change.

The people whose stories you just read are, tragically, the minority among the wrongfully convicted.

They got their lives back.

Though it's impossible to know for sure how many innocent people are in prison, studies have estimated that between 2.3 and 5 percent of inmates in the United States are innocent. That could put the number of the wrongfully convicted as high as one hundred thousand.

Most of these people will serve their sentences to the end. This may happen because they've given up fighting or, more likely, because their fight is unwinnable for any number of reasons—the evidence was lost or destroyed, the fraudulent accuser refuses to recant, or they can't find a lawyer to take their case.

It needs to stop. But how?

"You need to change the ethic in the prosecutor's office from being *winning at all costs* to what the rules of professional conduct say the prosecutor is, which is a minister of justice," says Steve Kaplan, the Minneapolis attorney whose client Damon Thibodeaux sat on Louisiana death row for fifteen years before he got out.

"I think they all go in with great intentions, but the fact of the matter is they're political animals and they're judged on their wins and losses. So I think you've got to get the politics out of it and you've got to have prosecutors who will say to their people, 'I will not judge you on your wins and losses. I will judge you on the quality of justice you dispense.'"

A change in attitude doesn't happen on its own. The Innocence Project, which carries the banner in the fight against wrongful convictions, has—along with other groups—called for legislation to reduce the number of innocent people being convicted in the first place.

The good news is the tide is starting to shift. Reforms are slowly but steadily emerging to overhaul the five most common causes of wrongful conviction: false confessions, eyewitness misidentification, improper forensic science, false accusations, and government misconduct.

FALSE CONFESSIONS

As of 2014, 13 percent of the exonerees on the National Registry of Exonerations went to prison because they confessed to crimes they didn't commit. They might have been mentally impaired or intoxicated when they confessed. They might have confessed because they were ignorant of the law. Or, as in the case of Damon Thibodeaux, they confessed because cops gave them no other choice.

When detectives interrogated Thibodeaux, they employed the Reid Technique, which involves steps devised to convince the suspect that there's so much evidence against him that his case is hopeless. So if he has any sense at all, he'd better fess up. "You're at their mercy in the broadest sense," says Steve Kaplan. "What happens to you in that room is entirely up to them. There are no checks and balances."

It took nine hours before Thibodeaux finally cracked. He picked up on what they wanted him to say because they were feeding him crime scene information. He just repeated it all back to them. When the crime lab came back with the results, it was obvious that everything Thibodeaux confessed about the murder was wrong. Yet at no point did they go back and say, "Maybe we have a false confession here."

They charged him with capital murder instead.

Had the entire interrogation been recorded—and then brought to trial, where the defense lawyer would turn it into mincemeat, if the judge didn't toss it first—Thibodeaux may well have avoided prison time. Instead, the false confession played the key role in getting him convicted.

Innocence advocates say the best way to bring down the number of false confessions is to record the interrogations in their entirety. The reason is simple: police know that if the record shows they coerced the suspect or made him regurgitate details of the crime—or, for that matter, beat the confession out of him—the confession would get tossed out.

More than 850 jurisdictions across the country regularly record police interrogations, according to the Innocence Project. Most do so because they are required by law. But some jurisdictions, such as Broward County, Florida, and Santa Clara County, California, have taken on the measure because it's just good policing. It not only protects the innocent, but makes authentic confessions more reliable.

EYEWITNESS MISIDENTIFICATION

According to the Registry, some 35 percent of the exonerated were wrongfully convicted because of mistaken eyewitness identification.

"There is no more powerful evidence than a sympathetic, traumatized victim pointing a finger at the defendant and saying, 'I'm absolutely positive that that is the man who assaulted me. I will never forget his face for as long as I live,'" says Nina Morrison, the senior attorney with the Innocence Project and the lawyer who represented Cornelius Dupree.

Dupree was just a teenager when he got picked up by a police officer at a checkpoint in Dallas. A woman and her boyfriend identified him as a rapist, and that was all it took for him to get convicted—even though the boyfriend did not initially identify Dupree at the police station.

Since 1981, Dallas police departments have made great strides in changing the way they do lineups, namely implementing the sequential double-blind procedure. During this procedure, neither the witness nor the administrator of the lineup knows who the suspect is. Lineup members appear sequentially instead of all at once. This has proven to greatly reduce the risk of witness misidentification. Had such measures been in effect in 1979, Dupree might not have lost more than thirty years of his life.

Unfortunately, many police departments continue to use traditional live and photo lineups in which the administrator knows who the suspect is. Often, the administrator does not properly instruct the witness, which leads to mistakes.

The Innocence Projects suggests several simple procedures that would reduce the number of misidentifications:

Making sure everyone in the lineup, not just the suspect, resembles the witness's description of the perpetrator

Informing the witness that the perpetrator may not be in the lineup at all, but the investigation will continue regardless

Having the witness produce a statement after the lineup is over, in which he indicates his level of confidence in the identification

Acceptance of such reforms has been slow. Yet states like Wisconsin, New Jersey, and North Carolina have implemented some, and have found them to be highly effective in keeping innocent people from being charged.

IMPROPER FORENSIC SCIENCE

Improper forensic science contributed to the imprisonment of 22 percent of those listed on the Registry. This often occurs because the forensic techniques have not been rigorously tested or the testing itself is inaccurate.

Much of the reason James Kluppelberg was found guilty of setting the fire that killed most of a family was due to the testimony of a fire department captain. He stated that the burn patterns he noticed at the fire scene bore the markings of arson. This would be wholly disproved nearly a quarter century later.

"He had testimony that I would characterize as junk science," says one of his attorneys Gayle Horn, of the Chicago firm Loevy & Loevy and founding member of the Exoneration Project at the University of Chicago Law School. "Certainly nobody's standing behind it now. It's been debunked by the current understanding of how arson works. But even at the time, that wasn't really a valid analysis."

Captain Francis Burns of the Chicago Fire Department had taken no notes and made no reports, yet he testified with authority that the fire was arson. This was in spite of investigators concluding that the cause couldn't be determined.

"It's unfortunate that there was somebody from fire investigation who disregarded that conclusion and fabricated arson evidence suggesting that the cause of the fire was incendiary," Horn says.

The Innocence Project and the National Academy of Sciences have recommended the establishment of a national forensic science agency that would have comparable authority to the Food and Drug Association. It would, among other things, set scientific standards in the forensics field, oversee research, and provide certifications for forensic laboratories and practitioners.

A good first step toward this goal is already in the works. In 2013, the Department of Justice and the National Institute of Standards and Technology established the first National Commission on Forensic Science. This commission is a thirty-member committee of forensic scientists, judges, prosecutors, and defense attorneys who will develop policy recommendations for the US Attorney General.

And in 2014, two US senators introduced separate bills that would improve forensic science reform efforts. The Forensic Science and Standards Act of 2014 and the Criminal Justice and Forensic Science Reform Act would develop and implement uniform standards for forensics. It would also promote stronger oversight for forensic laboratories and practitioners. With these improvements to forensic standards, the accused have a better shot at a fair trial.

FALSE ACCUSATION OR PERJURY

A staggering 57 percent of the exonerees listed on the Registry went to prison because someone falsely accused them of committing a crime. In many instances, the accusers were jailhouse snitches who lied under oath in exchange for leniency in their own cases.

When jailbird Greg Gully falsely testified that he'd heard Kerry Porter admit to killing a truck driver in cold blood, the jury bought it. In their eyes, Gully's words amounted to a confession from Porter himself.

"Even though we know from empirical data that confessions are sometimes false, if they're incredibly persuasive, you have to ask, 'Why would somebody say they did it if they didn't?'" says Porter's attorney Melanie Lowe, from the Kentucky Innocence Project. "This was the nastiest version of that. It was filtered through someone the prosecution presented as having no motive to lie. We found he had every reason to lie."

Greg Gully was a confidential informant who snitched on inmates for several different agencies. None of this was mentioned at Porter's trial because Gully's identity wasn't known even by Porter's public defender.

"He was very believable to the jury because they thought he was just a guy that happened to be in jail, that knew the victim and took it upon himself to get this information," Lowe says. "And that's the one thing the jury found the most persuasive when they were polled after the case."

States have been slow to pass laws preventing jailhouse snitches from wielding such influence in the courtroom. But a few have made great strides. For instance, in 2011, California Governor Jerry Brown signed a bill preventing judges and juries from relying solely on the testimony of jailhouse snitches. The law requires prosecutors to either present forensic evidence or corroborate the snitch's testimony with that of other inmate witnesses.

OFFICIAL MISCONDUCT

Misconduct by police or prosecutors had a role in the convictions of 47 percent of the exonerees on the Registry, as well as nearly all the exonerees profiled in this book.

Prosecutorial misconduct includes withholding exculpatory evidence from the defense, destroying evidence, and allowing unreliable witnesses or fraudulent experts to testify. Police misconduct includes coercing false confessions, lying on the witness stand, or failing to turn over evidence to prosecutors.

Devon Ayers, the Bronx teen wrongfully convicted of murdering a Federal Express employee and a livery cab driver, was a classic victim of unfair and overly aggressive law enforcement practices. Ayers might not have done eighteen years in prison had the police turned over a crucial surveillance video that discredited one of the key witnesses. And, while researching his case, Ayers's legal team discovered that the police had also fed crime scene details to two drug-addict witnesses to help them "recollect" what they'd seen.

"The weakness of the evidence was a huge problem and the quality of the witnesses was a big problem and something that gave us a big concern," says Ayers's lawyer Glenn Garber, founder and director of the New York City-based Exoneration Initiative.

"You're talking about witnesses who have their stories changed and developed as the police investigation went on. And these were witnesses that were very malleable, and what they were testifying to was [overhearing] admissions [of guilt] by the defendant—which is the weakest evidence that you can encounter.

"The jury has to discredit the cops to dismiss that evidence. It's very insidious. It gives police a tremendous amount of power."

Changing the ethic in law enforcement is incredibly difficult, but there has been some movement. Since 2000, eleven states have implemented criminal justice reform commissions that are specifically geared to study wrongful convictions and how to change the system. These states include North Carolina, Illinois, Pennsylvania, Florida, and New York.

WHAT CAN WE DO?
Make a hell of a lot of noise.

Perhaps the stories in this book moved you or made you angry. Now take those feelings and let the Powers That Be hear it.

The best thing going right now for the wrongfully convicted is momentum. In recent years, a seemingly endless stream of exoneration stories continues to be covered by the media. Being in the limelight hastens the kinds of positive changes we've seen, like police departments shifting the way they do lineups and interrogations, introduction of new legislation to improve standards in forensics, and states forming commissions to study wrongful convictions.

That's a good start, but there's a long, long way to go. Experts have suggested some ways the average person can help.

When you read a news article about someone who has been exonerated, post the story on social media, write a comment in the article's comments section, and email the journalist to thank him or her. When media companies see certain stories getting a big response, they're more likely to keep those stories coming. That keeps wrongful convictions in the spotlight and keeps pressure on the politicians to make things right.

Research local law enforcement practices. If your feeling is that they're not up to snuff, let your elected officials know. You can also express your concerns at local civic group meetings.

See how you can volunteer. Innocence organizations work on shoestring budgets. They typically need thousands of volunteer hours to get just one inmate out of prison. You can see which innocence groups are in your state by visiting www.innocencenetwork.org. Contact them and find out how you can help. And, of course, these groups are always in need of donations.

Educate yourself and those around you. This book hopefully gave you a cursory understanding of the issues, but there is always more to learn. Ultimately, educating ourselves and each other will have the greatest impact. Because during a criminal trial, neither the prosecutors nor defense lawyers are the ones deciding who goes to prison and who walks free. It's up to the jury.

One day, you could be on a jury that makes such a decision. But if you know nothing about how litigation works, then you can easily be seduced by whichever counsel is the shrewdest and best prepared. So be skeptical. Lawyers on both sides are motivated and paid to win, whether or not the defendant is innocent or guilty.

It's not a fair fight unless we make it fair.

RESOURCES

Here are some useful resources for finding out more about efforts to help the wrongfully convicted:

The Innocence Network
http://www.innocencenetwork.org

The Innocence Project
http://www.innocenceproject.org

The National Registry of Exonerations
https://www.law.umich.edu/special/exoneration/Pages/about.aspx

NOTES

CHAPTER 1: DAMON THIBODEAUX
1. Erin Moriarty, "The Confession of Damon Thibodeaux," 48 Hours, http://www.cbsnews.com/news/the-confession-of-damon-thibodeaux/
2. Douglas A. Blackmon, "Louisiana Death-Row Inmate Damon Thibodeaux Exonerated with DNA Evidence," *Washington Post*, http://www.washingtonpost.com/national/louisiana-death-row-inmate-damon-thibodeaux-is-exonerated-with-dna-evidence/2012/09/28/26e30012-0997-11e2-afff-d6c7f20a83bf_story.html
3. Ibid.
4: Ed Pilkington, "Louisiana Death Row Inmate Freed after 15 Years——with a Little Help from DNA," *Guardian*, http://www.theguardian.com/world/2012/dec/07/

dna-testing-frees-man-death-row

CHAPTER 2: JAMES KLUPPELBERG
1. People v. Kluppelberg, 628 N.E.2d 908 (Ill. App. Ct. 1993)

CHAPTER 3: DEBRA BROWN
1. Justin Higginbottom, "Shadow of Guilt," *Salt Lake City Weekly*, http://www.cityweekly.net/utah/shadow-of-guilt/Content?oid=2287559
2. Ibid.

CHAPTER 4: CORNELIUS DUPREE
1. Jennifer Emily, "'It's a Joy to Be Free Again,' Says Exoneree Who Served 30 Years in Dallas Robbery, Rape," *Dallas Morning News*, http://www.dallasnews.com/news/crime/headlines/20110105-it_s-a-joy-to-be-free-again_says-exoneree-who-served-30-years-in-dallas-robbery-rape.ece

CHAPTER 5: DRAYTON WITT
1. Lewis Roca Rothgerber: Randy Papetti, "State of Arizona vs. Drayton Shawn Witt: Exhibits," 2014, http://www.lrrlaw.com/randy-papetti/#.VMAqn4vF9DC
2. Ibid.
3. Ibid.
4. Richard Ruelas, "Innocent Dad Won't Face Retrial in Death of Baby," *Arizona Republic*, November 1, 2012.

CHAPTER 7: THOMAS KENNEDY
1. "Falsely Accused and Convicted," YouTube video, 42:52, interview from an episode of *Katie* televised by ABC, posted by "MightyFalcon2011," May 21, 2013, http://www.youtube.com/watch?v=IfftiISeIi0
2. Tony Lystra, "Local Girl Lied about 2001 Rape; Father

Set Free," *The Daily News Online*, http://tdn.com/news/
local/local-girl-lied-about-rape-father-set-free/article_
bf9cac36-7c7a-11e1-a9e4-001a4bcf887a.html

CHAPTER 8: KERRY PORTER

1. Andrew Wolfson, "Conviction Fails to End Questions,"
Louisville Courier-Journal, http://archive.courier-journal.
com/article/20111024/NEWS01/310240010

2. Ibid.

3. ---, "Prosecutors Say They are Moving to Clear Convicted
Murderer," *Louisville Courier-Journal*, http://archive.cou-
rier-journal.com/article/20110831/NEWS01/308310078/
Prosecutors-say-they-moving-clear-convicted-murderer

4. "Families of Victim, Killer Unite for Justice," WLKY Louisville, http://www.wlky.com/
Families-Of-Victim-Killer-Unite-For-Justice/9786080

5. Ibid.

6. Andrew Wolfson, "Kerry Porter, Imprisoned
for Murder, is Exonerated, Freed after 14 Years,"
Louisville Courier-Journal, http://archive.courier-jour-
nal.com/article/20111219/NEWS01/312190066/
Kerry-Porter-murder-Tyrone-Camp

7. Ibid.

8. "Man Back Home After Being Exonerated from
Murder Conviction," WLKY Louisville, http://www.
wlky.com/Man-Back-Home-After-Being-Exonerat-
ed-From-Murder-Conviction/10025944

9. Ibid.

CHAPTER 9: VIRGINIA LeFEVER

1. "Woman Innocent? A Woman Says Her Mother is
Guilty of Poisoning Her Father," 10 Investigates video, 3:14,
from a newscast televised by WBNS-10TV Columbus,
Ohio, November 24, 2010, http://www.10tv.com/content/

sections/video/index.html?video=/videos/2010/11/24/
woman-innocent.xml

2. Jesse Balmert, "Virginia LeFever Sues Officials Over
False Imprisonment," *Newark Advocate* (Ohio), October
19, 2011.

3. --- , "Virginia LeFever Murder Case Dismissed,"
Newark Advocate (Ohio), April 22, 2011.

4. Josh Jarman, "'Faulty Science' Raises Doubts; Toxicologist Who Lied Might Have Been Key in Other Ohio
Convictions," *Columbus Dispatch,* May 11, 2011.

CHAPTER 10: DEVON AYERS

1. Michael O. Allen and Jose Lambiet, "'Wanted' Kill
Suspect Surrenders," *New York Daily News*, March 17,
1995.

In addition to the sources listed here, the research for
this book is based on hundreds of hours of interviews
with exonerees and lawyers, as well as the examination of
numerous court documents, transcripts, and news items
related to the cases.

ACKNOWLEDGMENTS

This book would not exist if ten incredible men and women had not invited me into their lives to let me tell their stories. Cornelius Dupree, Devon Ayers, Ginny LeFever, Damon Thibodeaux, James Kluppelberg, Drayton Witt, Thomas Kennedy, Debra Brown, Muhammad Don Ray Adams, and Kerry Porter: With all my heart, I thank you.

I am deeply indebted to the lawyers who freed the ten, and who gave me so much valuable insight and guidance as I wrote this book. They are Nina Morrison, Glenn Garber, Kort Gatterdam, Steve Kaplan, Gayle Horn, Randy Papetti, Terry Mulligan, Jensie Anderson, Penny Marshall, and Melanie Lowe.

And a special thanks to Paul Cates, a lawyer from the Innocence Project, who came through for me more times than I can count.

I'm eternally grateful to Dr. Rubin "Hurricane" Carter, a crusader for the wrongfully convicted, who wrote the foreword to this book a month before cancer took his life. May he rest in peace.

Equal thanks go to Ken Klonsky, the middleman who—racing against the clock—managed to coax the abovementioned foreword out of his friend Dr. Carter. I don't know how you pulled it off, Ken, and I will never forget it.

It's nearly impossible to get a book published without a good literary agent. I've got a fantastic one: Bob Diforio of D4EO Literary Agency. Thank you, Bob.

And thank you to my excellent editor, Karen Ang, for helping me find the assertive voice that this book badly needed. That, and your painstaking revisions, made all the difference.

I could not have asked for a better publisher than Tantor. Thank you, Hilary Eurich, Ron Formica, Allan Hoving, John Molish, Cassandra McNeil, and Suzanne Mitchell, for your professionalism and fine work.

My skills as a journalist were not self-taught. I never could have pulled off this book without first being trained by the amazing staff at the *New York Post*. My gratitude, in particular, goes to Michelle Gotthelf, Dan Greenfield, Neil Sloane, and Eric Lenkowitz.

One other mentor I must thank is my good friend Matthew Lysiak, who guided me along this journey from the very beginning, starting with the lesson, "The future favors the bold."

My warmest thanks go to my wife Brocha, for her invaluable read-throughs, on-the-ball suggestions, and limitless love and support. And to my sons Marty and Daniel, who always make me want to do better.

ABOUT THE AUTHOR

Reuven Fenton has been covering murder and scandal for the *New York Post* since 2007, and has earned national recognition for his exclusive reporting on a myriad of national stories. Mr. Fenton was inspired to write *Stolen Years* after covering an unforgettable court hearing in 2013, in which a Brooklyn judge freed David Ranta, who had been wrongfully convicted for murdering a rabbi twenty-two years earlier. The sensational story sparked an investigation into misconduct by both the Brooklyn District Attorney's Office and the lead detective in the case. Mr. Fenton is a graduate of Columbia University School of Journalism, and lives in New York City with his wife and two sons. Follow @reuvenfen on Twitter.